How to Lead It: Primary Maths

Other titles from Bloomsbury Education

How to Lead It: Primary English by Tricia Moss and Sallie Stanton

How to Lead It: Primary Science by Kirsty Simkin

How to Lead It: Primary History by Alex Pethick

How to Lead It: Primary Geography by Emma Lennard

How to Lead It: Primary Art and Design by Naomi Pilling

The Curriculum Compendium by Rae Snape

What Every Teacher Needs to Know by Jade Pearce

How to Lead It: Primary Maths

Shannen Doherty
Series editor: Jon Hutchinson

BLOOMSBURY EDUCATION
LONDON OXFORD NEW YORK NEW DELHI SYDNEY

BLOOMSBURY EDUCATION
Bloomsbury Publishing Plc
50 Bedford Square, London WC1B 3DP, UK
Bloomsbury Publishing Ireland Limited
29 Earlsfort Terrace, Dublin 2, D02 AY28, Ireland

BLOOMSBURY, BLOOMSBURY EDUCATION and the Diana logo are trademarks of Bloomsbury Publishing Plc

First published in Great Britain, 2026 by Bloomsbury Publishing Plc
This edition published in Great Britain, 2026 by Bloomsbury Publishing Plc

A catalogue record for this book is available from the British Library

ISBN: PB: 978-1-80199-471-2; ePub: 978-1-80199-472-9

2 4 6 8 10 9 7 5 3 1 (paperback)

Cover design by Sophie Gordon

Typeset by Lumina Datamatics Ltd
Printed and bound in Great Britain by TJ Books, Padstow, Cornwall

FSC www.fsc.org MIX Paper | Supporting responsible forestry FSC® C013056

To find out more about our authors and books, visit www.bloomsbury.com and sign up for our newsletters.

For product safety-related questions, contact productsafety@bloomsbury.com.

Contents

1 Leading maths

Leading primary maths is one of the most exciting roles you can take on in school. Whether you're stepping into subject leadership for the first time, building on previous experience or even looking ahead to the future, this book is designed to inspire you, challenge you and make you think.

From the moment I started my teacher training, I aspired to become a maths subject leader. I knew I wanted to share my love and enjoyment of the subject with colleagues, but I also knew I needed to understand the complexities and challenges of being a subject leader, especially of a core subject like maths. I've spent years exploring how to make maths teaching accessible, effective and exciting for every pupil. From leading my own school's curriculum to supporting others in refining theirs, I've learned a lot of lessons along the way!

This chapter will explore the importance of maths in primary education, the National Curriculum in England and what it says about maths, the role of a maths leader and how this differs to leading other subjects, and the key end points and outcomes in primary maths.

The importance of maths in primary education

Maths is a cornerstone of primary education. It is vital that we get it right!

Early interactions with maths, such as recognising pattern, understanding shape and counting, are crucial in developing a sense of number. When pupils engage in mathematically-rich tasks from a young age, it lays the foundation for encountering number later on, prepares them to tackle more complex concepts as they progress through school, and promotes positive attitudes towards the subject.

A strong foundation in maths can lead to success and enjoyment in STEM (science, technology, engineering and maths) subjects and other subjects like geography. In an average primary school year, pupils will participate in daily maths lessons, weekly science lessons, and regular DT and geography lessons. Coming to these lessons with the appropriate knowledge of number, statistics, shape and measure will increase success and therefore motivation.

In addition to all of the above, maths is fun. We have the huge privilege of teaching maths to our pupils every day and showing them just how interesting it can be. While I'm not suggesting we make every maths lesson into a party, we can absolutely make sure pupils enjoy what they are learning.

Understanding the primary maths curriculum

Looking at the aims and component parts of primary maths can give us more context on our role as the maths subject leader. Effective primary maths teaching is likely to have many of the same principles and practices, but the specifics of different countries' curriculums may vary. As a subject leader, your role requires you to be well versed in the curriculum to ensure your school is meeting its statutory obligations. Let's consider the National Curriculum in England (DfE, 2013) as an example. This has evolved over three decades and is the result of experts in maths thinking deeply about the why, what and how of maths teaching and learning.

The Purpose of Study says:

> *'Mathematics is a creative and highly interconnected discipline that has been developed over centuries, providing the solution to some of history's most intriguing problems. It is essential to everyday life, critical to science, technology and engineering, and necessary for financial literacy and most forms of employment. A high-quality mathematics education therefore provides a foundation for understanding the world, the ability to reason mathematically, an appreciation of the beauty and power of mathematics, and a sense of enjoyment and curiosity about the subject.'*
>
> (DfE, 2013, p. 99)

If we are honest about our teaching practice, I wonder how often we push 'the beauty and power of mathematics' in a world where we have a limited time to impart a lot of knowledge. If we can see our curriculum through the lens of maths' beauty and power, we can create opportunities and experiences that will foster that 'sense of enjoyment and curiosity'. Maths truly is a beautiful subject. Look at Fibonacci spirals in nature, the symmetry of snowflakes or the fractals in the fronds of a fern. There is so much good to unpack in our curriculum and it is your role as a subject leader to demonstrate this to your staff, pupils and families. We know that there is a lot to teach, but if we rush through like a never-ending conveyor belt, we run the risk of missing the best bits. We should be empowering our teachers and their pupils to hit pause every so often and really dig into the beauty of the subject. The National Curriculum in England seeks to make pupils:

- fluent in the fundamentals of mathematics through varied practice that develops conceptual understanding
- able to reason mathematically through conjecturing, generalising, justifying and using mathematical language
- able to solve routine and non-routine problems by using a range of approaches (DfE, 2013).

It is important that you have a clear understanding of these terms as a maths subject leader so that your colleagues can be just as clear. You will want to consider how you approach these areas both in your curriculum and in the day-to-day teaching of maths. These areas each have their own chapter later, but it is worth us defining the terms now before we consider how best to develop them in our own schools.

Fluency

At its heart, fluency is the ability to manipulate number and apply skills in multiple contexts. It's also about being able to select the most appropriate method from a toolkit of approaches to solve calculations. We are in danger of fluency becoming synonymous with the rapid recall of facts, which is undoubtedly important to mathematical understanding, but not the most important.

Reasoning

Reasoning involves thinking mathematically, using what is already known to make logical links to solve problems. In a blog about fluency, reasoning and problem solving, Neil Almond (2025b) said, 'mathematical reasoning is the bridge between fluency and problem solving. It allows pupils to use the former to accurately carry out the latter.'

It is vital that we don't see reasoning as just a question that requires an explanation, or worse a selection of questions that only the pupils with high prior attainment can answer in a lesson. Reasoning is not a style of question. It is a way of thinking and working to solve problems that can be developed in every pupil.

Problem solving

Just as with fluency and reasoning, there are misconceptions around what problem solving is in maths too. Problem solving is not just 'word problems'. In fact, these often test fluency, for example a 'problem' like *Jamie has baked 25 cookies. Luca has baked 17. How many more cookies has Jamie baked than Luca?* This word problem requires pupils to see the structure of 25-17 within the question rather than requiring a particular problem-solving strategy. Problem solving is how we apply conceptual understanding and procedural fluency to answer unfamiliar problems.

Foster (2019) demonstrates his view of how problem solving relates to fluency and reasoning in his pyramid model where fluency in facts, procedures and concepts sits at the bottom, with mathematical reasoning above it and problem solving at the top.

Problem solving is 'the most important goal of all' (p. 8), but this doesn't mean that fluency and reasoning are to be sped through to get to problem solving. Fluency is the foundation of mathematical reasoning and problem solving, and therefore deserves time to be learned and practised to automaticity.

The role of a primary maths leader

Your role as a maths leader is a varied one and is often done alongside an almost full teaching timetable. Because of this, the task can feel overwhelming at times. It is always worth reminding yourself that you aren't a superhero, and you have limited time, so don't be hard on yourself! Hopefully, you can relish the chance to have a strategic vision over the direction of maths in your school and enjoy the role.

Mary Kennedy (2016) identifies five persistent problems that teachers face: portraying the curriculum, enlisting student participation, exposing student thinking, containing student behaviour and accommodating personal needs. These are problems that teachers face continually and are never completely 'done'. As a maths leader, you might consider what your own persistent problems are. These are likely to be the same, or similar, for every maths leader, regardless of where your school is, what has been done up until now or what is on your school improvement/development plan. Potential areas for persistent problems might be:

- curriculum development
- resourcing
- monitoring teaching and learning
- supporting colleagues.

Curriculum development

The maths leader is the person in school who will design or choose a curriculum or scheme of work. Alongside senior leaders and teaching staff, decisions around curriculum come to you. You may have an embedded scheme of work, written your own curriculum, need a new scheme of work or want to supplement your current curriculum with additional resources. Whichever position you are in, you will want to know what is going well, and what does and doesn't work for teachers and pupils about the current curriculum. Even an embedded curriculum or scheme of work needs reviewing and adjusting to meet the changing needs of the school.

In Chapter 4, we will consider how your role as a subject leader impacts the organisation and progression of the curriculum and timetabling decisions. While there are lots of subjects to teach, we want maths to have the profile in school that it deserves!

A huge part of curriculum development work maths leaders do is developing the subject knowledge of teachers and teaching assistants (TAs) so that they can confidently and effectively deliver the curriculum and support pupils' learning. There may be gaps in knowledge because of a change in a scheme of work or a change in staff, and your role requires you to train staff to put them in the best position possible for your pupils. Subject knowledge might be understanding the big objectives, breaking them apart into small steps and understanding how they connect to other parts of the curriculum, or it might go right down to the specifics of which representation or method to use based on what others use across the school.

Resourcing

For teachers to feel able to teach and pupils able to learn, we need to ensure that they are well-equipped for them to do so. As a primary maths subject leader, managing resources is a vital aspect of your role in ensuring high-quality teaching and learning across the school.

Resources could be physical or online. Here are some of the resources you could be responsible for managing:

- manipulatives
- textbooks
- online maths learning platforms
- online quizzing platforms
- teacher-facing websites
- online testbases.

It is likely that you will be responsible for ordering resources that align with the curriculum and support effective pedagogy. It can be tempting to go onto education resource websites and order one of everything, but you will want to sit with your teachers and discuss the key resources that are needed. Instead of a scattergun approach, think about what you want your pupils exposed to throughout their primary school experience.

You will also need to consider how best to organise these resources. Will they be in classrooms? Is there a maths cupboard? Do you need to store some resources in classrooms as they will be used more frequently and others in a cupboard for particular topics? Clear, accessible storage systems can empower teachers to use resources confidently and efficiently.

It is not enough to just order and organise resources. We must ensure that our teachers and teaching assistants know how to use them. Make them part of your regular maths professional development (PD) sessions so that teachers can see them in action. For example, when delivering PD on teaching place value in numbers with up to four-digits, ensure each table of teachers has base 10 equipment to manipulate in the session, building and partitioning numbers with up to four-digits. Or, when training staff on teaching multiplying fractions, demonstrate to them how to fold a piece of paper to show this.

Monitoring teaching and learning

'Monitoring' can feel like a loaded word depending on how you and your colleagues have experienced it in the past. It is vital that monitoring activities are done with the intention of evaluating the *impact* of the curriculum, teaching and assessment to improve the learning for the pupils in your school. It is worth discussing this with your senior leaders. It could be argued that replacing the term 'monitoring' with 'evaluation' might send the right message to staff. Across each term, you are likely to conduct learning walks, pupil voice, teacher voice and book looks with pupils or teachers. These should always be done in a supportive and developmental manner. 'What can I learn from this?' is a key question to keep asking yourself so that it informs your next moves and develops you as a leader. Monitoring, or evaluating, teaching and learning is never about checking up on staff or telling them off; it is about understanding what is going on in your subject and school.

You may want to ask staff or parents and carers to facilitate their children completing an online pupil voice survey to get a range of responses. This might look something like Figure 1.1.

	Strongly agree	Agree	Not sure	Disagree	Strongly disagree
I enjoy maths lessons.	○	○	○	○	○
Maths is an important subject.	○	○	○	○	○
I understand what I am learning in maths.	○	○	○	○	○
My teacher sets challenging tasks.	○	○	○	○	○
I know what to do when I am stuck.	○	○	○	○	○
I feel like I am making good progress in maths.	○	○	○	○	○

Figure 1.1 Example pupil-voice survey

The benefit of an online survey is that the results are collated for you, and you can begin to look at the spread of answers across year groups or the school, which might look like Figure 1.2.

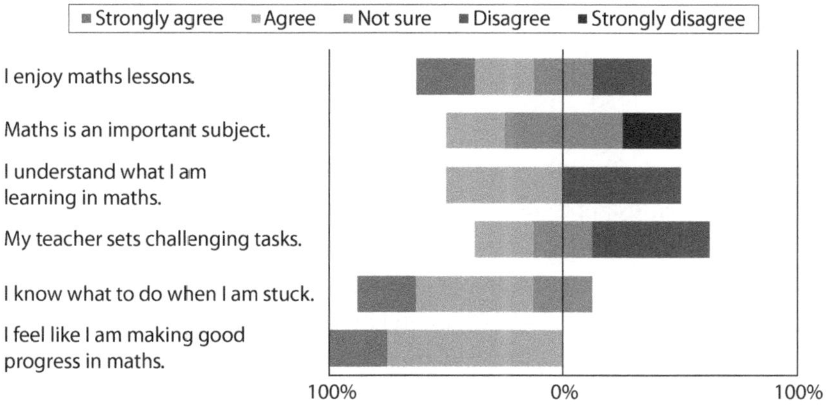

Figure 1.2 Bar chart showing results of pupil-voice survey

While an online survey definitely has a purpose, it is also worth doing more in-depth pupil voice with small focus groups from across the school. Here are some example pupil voice questions:

- What does a typical maths lesson look like?
- Can you show me something you are proud of in your maths book?
- What have you learned recently?
- Do you think you are getting better at maths?
- What do you enjoy about maths lessons?
- Is there anything that you don't enjoy?
- How do you get help when you are stuck in maths?
- How do you know you are doing well in maths lessons?
- What does your teacher do to help you learn more?

The answers to these questions can lead to rich discussions with pupils from Early Years Foundation Stage (EYFS) up to Year 6; they will give you more specific feedback than just an online survey and they will inform your next steps for PD. In your next maths PD session, you could have a slide on the screen sharing a few quotes from across the school as your colleagues arrive – this generally puts a smile on people's faces because we all know children come out with the best things!

Supporting colleagues

Effective subject leaders empower their colleagues to be more effective teachers. You can draw from a range of methods for supporting colleagues: whole staff professional development, coaching, training, collaborative planning or team-teaching. Each of these will serve a purpose to improve maths teaching and learning in your school.

You will, hopefully, have plenty of opportunities to lead professional development sessions with your colleagues linked to your subject development plan, and there are examples of how to structure PD sessions throughout the book.

You might also develop a coaching model for maths teaching where you drop into lessons focusing on an agreed area and then engage in a coaching conversation with the teacher. By focusing on bite-sized, incremental changes that feed into a wider goal, you can improve a teacher's practice at a greater pace than if you were only delivering whole-staff training.

In some cases, you might join planning, preparation and assessment (PPA) sessions with other year groups so that you can model effective planning and preparation, and collaborate with your colleagues in a more focused environment. You may also then work with particular teachers through team-teaching where you go into their classrooms and teach alongside them.

The big O

I won't say too much about Ofsted, because this book isn't a guide to get you through an inspection! However, it would be silly not to mention Ofsted. No doubt Ofsted will be on your mind as a subject lead. However, having been through multiple inspections, I can honestly say that the best way to prepare for Ofsted is to know your subject well, understand how your subject is enacted and understand the impact being achieved. That's exactly what this book aims to provide guidance with.

Interview on the role of a maths leader – Louise McLaughlin

Louise is an experienced senior leader and primary maths leader having worked in schools in London, Surrey and East Sussex.

Working as a maths subject lead is a joy and a privilege. The subject is high-stakes and should be high profile in any school, so it needs careful and constant attention. The main purpose of the role is to provide leadership and management for maths in order to secure high-quality teaching of a clear and robust maths curriculum, making effective use of resources so that standards are raised and outcomes are improved. Basically – find out how well maths is being taught and learned, and then make these two things even better!

I have been the maths subject lead in my current school for almost a year. The first thing I did when joining the school and taking on the role was to create a baseline. I needed to get to know what was happening with maths across the school. This took the form of looking at the school improvement plan and the maths action plan, as well as a document known as the school's 'guide' to maths. We plan and teach from the

White Rose curriculum scheme, which ensures that we are covering the National Curriculum objectives for maths across the school from EYFS to Year 6. I already knew that outcomes were below the nationally expected standard for attainment in maths, and I analysed the school's most recent maths attainment and progress data to find out more and identify any particular areas of focus.

Once I had this high-level overview, I was able to start the job of action planning to move forwards. It is an integral part of leading the subject to be able to work with senior leaders confidently and effectively. I maintain communication with the senior leadership team (SLT) over what is happening with maths at our school, which has led to a relationship of trust. The leaders know that I am a proactive leader, and I know that they will support my work. One of my main foci has been providing clarity over the timetabling and lesson planning expectations for our teachers. There had been a different scheme used a few years ago, and some parts of the school's maths guide had become muddled. Teachers in our school now know exactly what to teach and when to teach it, including the additional fluency sessions which we have timetabled in order to develop pupils' numerical and computational skills appropriate to their age and stage.

During a typical term, I undertake a combination of leadership activities, such as leading subject knowledge and pedagogical knowledge development sessions with staff; talking to pupils about their maths learning; visiting lessons; and supporting planning. I use the school's monitoring schedule to plan my weekly activities and always make time for teachers to talk to me about maths. I am so passionate about the subject and am never too busy for a maths query!

One of the most easily overlooked but potentially very impactful aspects of maths leadership is, I would say, building and working with a network. I am lucky enough to work as part of a Multi-Academy Trust (MAT), so the maths network is well established, and I have built a relationship with the trust maths lead. However, I am also part of our geographically local maths hub, which provides great opportunities to share ideas and ask for support from people outside of your immediate sphere, who are likely faced with very similar challenges in their own schools. The importance of maths as a subject means that stakeholders will want and need to talk to you as a maths lead, so being able to talk about your subject in your school will always stand you in good stead.

Looking ahead, I want to help teachers to improve their approaches to adaptive teaching so that lessons are inclusive of children's varying needs and prior attainment. The maths curriculum is full and it can be hard to see the wood for the trees. It is essential that we focus on a mastery approach for all children so that the current gaps in attainment not only do not widen, but start to close. Every child can learn maths, and every teacher can love teaching it!

How this book can support you

Throughout this book, we will explore different aspects of primary maths provision in more detail, giving you a strong foundation from which to teach and lead the subject. You will find:

- examples of best practice across phases
- a mixture of fictional and real case studies for further exemplification
- suggestions for staff professional development
- reflection questions to help you structure your thoughts and identify next steps
- follow-up reading and resources if you want to explore a particular area further.

In the next chapter, we will draw together insights from cognitive science with evidence related to the practice of maths teaching. We then look at how you can take an evidence-based approach yourself.

In Chapter 3, we will look at maths mindsets at school and, in Chapter 4, maths curriculum design. You will then find detailed chapters on specific areas of the subject: fluency (Chapter 5), reasoning (Chapter 6) and problem solving (Chapter 7).

Next, we look at the importance of judiciously using models and representations (Chapter 8), variation (Chapter 9) and maths-based language (Chapter 10). Chapter 11 focusses on assessment in maths.

We will finish with guidance on ensuring consistency in your school's approaches (Chapter 12) and tips on implementing improvement and change (Chapter 13).

Questions for reflection

- What is the vision for maths at our school? How does this align with the wider curriculum vision?
- How do we communicate the beauty, power and enjoyment of maths to staff, pupils and families?
- How does attainment in maths compare with other subjects in our school, and nationally?

Explore further

- 'Becoming a maths lead' Chapter 23 of *Mastery in Primary Mathematics* (2020) by Tom Garry
- Ofsted's *Coordinating Mathematical Success: the Mathematics Subject Report* (2023)
- The National Centre for Excellence in the Teaching of Mathematics' *Taking on the Role of Maths Lead in a Primary School* (2022)

Chapter summary

- Maths is a cornerstone of primary education. It supports STEM and other subjects, with strong early experiences correlating to later achievement.
- Subject leaders should champion the enjoyment and beauty of the subject while ensuring that fluency, reasoning and problem solving are integral. We should consider how these three aims are defined and embedded, avoiding misconceptions and promoting their interconnected nature in teaching and learning.
- Leading primary maths gives you the chance to have a strategic vision for curriculum design, resource management, PD, mentoring and monitoring, ensuring a coherent and effective approach across the school.
- A good grasp of your subject and its delivery is essential when engaging with Ofsted or other accountability processes, even if this is not the sole focus of your role. You can use pupil and teacher voice, book looks and learning walks as tools to evaluate the impact of your subject.

2 Getting the best from research evidence

As a maths leader, engaging with research evidence is essential for making informed decisions that genuinely improve teaching and learning. However, in an age where educational research is abundant – and sometimes contradictory – it's easy to get lost in a sea of evidence. Worse still, confirmation bias can lead us to seek out only the research that aligns with what we already believe, rather than challenging our assumptions and refining our approach. This chapter will offer some guiding principles for engaging with education research, where you can find relevant research and evidence and how you might use it in your role as maths subject leader.

Guiding principles

As a maths leader, engaging with research evidence is crucial for driving improvements in teaching and learning. However, the way research is approached, interpreted and applied matters just as much as the research itself. You can't just consume research; it should be approached with a critical eye. By staying open to new things and evaluating research rigorously, you can create a culture of continuous improvement in your school. Navigating research can be confusing but, if you keep some guiding principles in mind, you can learn to apply it meaningfully and avoid common pitfalls.

Here are some key principles for making the most of educational research.

1. Be critical, not passive

Not all research is of equal quality. Some studies are robust and well-designed, while others may be based on limited samples, short-term effects or untested assumptions. Before adopting new ideas, ask:

- Who conducted the research, and what were their credentials?
- How large and diverse was the sample?
- Was the research peer-reviewed?
- Is the study relevant to our school's context?

2. Avoid confirmation bias

It's natural to seek out research that aligns with our existing beliefs, but true professional growth comes from engaging with perspectives that challenge our assumptions. Make a habit of reading research that contradicts or questions your school's current approaches, and encourage open discussion with colleagues about the strengths and weaknesses of different studies and how they relate to your values as educators.

3. Balance research with classroom experience

While research provides valuable insights, it must be balanced with the lived experiences of teachers and pupils. Educational theories may be compelling, but they need to be tested in real classrooms. Encourage teachers to trial research-informed strategies on a small scale, gather feedback and refine their approaches based on actual pupil responses.

4. Think long-term, not quick fixes

Educational trends come and go, often promising rapid improvements in pupil outcomes. However, sustainable change in maths teaching requires long-term thinking. Be wary of research that claims to offer 'silver bullet' solutions. Instead, focus on evidence-based strategies with a strong research foundation and a track record of success in different contexts.

5. Understand correlation vs. causation

Just because two things appear to be linked doesn't mean one causes the other. For example, research may show that high-performing pupils engage in more problem-solving activities, but this doesn't necessarily mean problem solving alone causes high attainment – it could be that confident pupils seek out challenges. Always question why research findings occur rather than assuming direct causation.

6. Engage with a range of sources

Relying on a single study or theory can lead to a narrow understanding of best practice. Instead, engage with a range of research sources, including:

- large-scale studies from organisations like the Education Endowment Foundation
- academic papers and systematic reviews
- insights from classroom practitioners and subject specialists
- government reports and curriculum research.

7. Foster a research-informed school culture

Research shouldn't just sit in the hands of leadership – it should be part of whole-school PD. Share key findings with staff in bite-sized, digestible formats, encourage discussion and create opportunities for teachers to engage with research through PD, lesson study, and collaborative projects.

8. Keep learning and questioning

The best subject leaders stay up to date with new research, attend conferences, participate in professional networks, and continuously question what works, why it works, and how it can be improved. By engaging with research critically and purposefully, you can ensure that evidence is used as a tool for meaningful improvement rather than an overwhelming collection of ideas that are difficult to implement.

Keep these principles in mind, but don't worry if it feels overwhelming to engage with research and evidence in this way. If you are new to the role or you haven't had much experience with educational research and evidence until this point, start by reading shorter blogs or articles. The piece on problem solving by Colin Foster (2019) referenced in Chapter 1 is a good place to start. From there, look at the reference list and set yourself a challenge to read the citations. You'll soon find yourself down a research rabbit hole! If you are hoping to read something longer, try to chunk it up and chip away at it over time. If you can find 15 minutes a day to read, e.g. in the morning with a cup of tea or coffee, you'll build the habit.

Primary education sources and guidance

There are many sources of research evidence available to maths leaders, so it's worth familiarising yourself with some key evidence bases.

Education Endowment Foundation (EEF)

The EEF offers large-scale, independent research reviews on teaching and learning strategies; the Teaching and Learning Toolkit, which summarises the impact of different approaches on attainment; guidance reports, including recommendations for teaching maths based on high-quality evidence; and research on metacognition, problem solving, fluency, and mathematical reasoning in primary education.

The Chartered College of Teaching

The Chartered College of Teaching offers the *Impact* Journal, summarising the latest research in education, including cognitive science and maths teaching; insights on assessment, memory, retrieval practice and curriculum sequencing; and case studies and practical guidance from teachers implementing research in real classrooms.

ResearchED

ResearchED is an organisation dedicated to closing the gap between educational research and classroom practice. It connects researchers, educators, and policymakers through conferences that often include subject-specific discussions. In addition to these events, ResearchED publishes concise books featuring insights from expert speakers, e.g. *The ResearchED Guide to Educational Myths or The ResearchED Guide to the Curriculum.*

Maths-specific resources

National Centre for Excellence in the Teaching of Mathematics (NCETM)

The NCETM offers research-based guidance on teaching for mastery, including the use of manipulatives (see Chapter 8) and variation theory (see Chapter 9); PD materials and case studies from Maths Hubs; deep dives into key mathematical concepts across the curriculum spine; and support for subject leaders in developing whole-school maths pedagogy.

Mathematical Association (MA)

The MA offers research papers on curriculum design, problem solving and reasoning; regular publications such as *Primary Mathematics Journal*, with research summaries and practical classroom applications; and resources on mathematical thinking and the history of mathematical education research.

Association of Teachers of Mathematics (ATM)

The ATM offers a strong focus on mathematical exploration, investigations and problem solving; research and articles on teaching mathematical reasoning and developing rich tasks; and PD materials and workshops informed by the latest educational research.

NRICH Maths

NRICH offers research-based problem-solving tasks and open-ended investigations; guidance on developing reasoning and mathematical thinking in all year groups; and articles on mathematical pedagogy and classroom implementation of research findings.

Blogs and podcasts

There are a number of education blogs and podcasts that you can catch up on and follow. Here are some key blogs to read and podcasts to listen to. They are not all primary maths focused, but they will all have something for you as maths leaders to dive into.

BLOGS	
Gareth Metcalfe: www.garethmetcalfe.wordpress.com	provides insights and resources on teaching primary maths, especially reasoning and problem solving
Sarah Farrell: www.mrsfclassroom.wordpress.com	discusses teaching primary maths and provides useful resources

Third Space Learning: https://thirdspacelearning.com/blog	provides resources and strategies for primary maths teaching and intervention from various contributors
Andrew Jeffery: https://andrewjeffrey.co.uk/	discusses practical resources and strategies for primary maths classrooms
Sophie Bartlett: www.missiebee1.wordpress.com	discusses a range of primary subjects and has specific blogs on teaching maths
Neil Almond: www.nutsaboutteaching.wordpress.com	discusses a range of primary-related issues and offers curriculum insights
Clare Sealy: www.primarytimery.com	explores topics on primary education, including oracy and curriculum development
Christopher Such: www.primarycolour.home.blog	shares resources and reflections on primary teaching
Elliot Morgan: www.mrmorgsthoughts.wordpress.com	reflects on primary education, including leadership, planning and assessment
Craig Barton: www.mrbartonmaths.com	mainly secondary-focused, offers insights on teaching maths and hosts a selection of research papers
Jo Morgan: www.resourceaholic.com	mainly secondary-focused and provides resources for teaching maths
Sarah Cottinghatt: www.overpractised.wordpress.com	provides insights on cognitive science and professional development
Tom Sherrington: www.teacherhead.com	discusses a range of issues in education and provides thoughts on professional development
Adam Boxer: www.achemicalorthodoxy.co.uk	secondary-focused insights on teaching and learning

PODCASTS	
Thinking Deeply about Primary Education	discusses a range of primary education topics with a focus on evidence-based practices
The NCETM Maths Podcast	covers developments and discussions in maths education
Mr Barton Maths Podcast	often secondary-focused interviews with educators discussing teaching methods and educational research
Tips for Teachers	provides practical teaching tips and strategies for educators
Primary Education Voices	shares stories and insights from primary education professionals
Mind the Gap	explores a range of topics in education through interviews and discussions

Education Research Reading Room	interviews with researchers and educators discussing their work
Evidence into Action	focuses on translating educational research into classroom practice
The Evidence Based Education Podcast	discusses the application of evidence in educational settings

Applying research to the role of maths leader

As a maths leader, your role involves more than just staying informed about current research; it's about applying that research in a way that aligns with the needs of your school and drives meaningful change. However, it's essential not to get distracted by every new finding but rather to focus on those that are most relevant and actionable for your context.

A needs-based approach is important when applying research to practice. Not all schools or classrooms are the same, and what works in one setting may not be as effective in another. As maths leader, your job is to assess the unique needs of your teachers and pupils and use research to inform strategies that will have the greatest impact. For example, if there are gaps in pupils' understanding of fundamental concepts like number sense or problem solving, then research-based interventions targeting these areas should take priority. Always evaluate your school's needs before jumping into broad implementation.

The best way to implement new ideas backed by research is through trial and evaluation. Instead of adopting a new strategy school-wide immediately, test it with a smaller group of teachers or a particular year group first. This allows you to assess the impact of the approach and refine it based on feedback and results. If the trial phase proves successful, you can begin to scale up, ensuring that the strategy is adapted and embedded effectively across the whole school. This incremental approach helps ensure that changes are sustainable and truly beneficial for both teachers and pupils.

Key research in primary maths teaching

Research in maths teaching has been instrumental in shaping effective pedagogical approaches and improving pupil outcomes. Over the years, educational researchers have made significant contributions that inform how we teach maths in primary schools.

Derek Haylock and structures

Derek Haylock's research and writings have been foundational in helping teachers better understand the structures and strategies behind teaching maths. His book *Mathematics Explained for Primary Teachers* (2024) is widely regarded as a key resource for primary maths teachers. Haylock emphasises the importance of developing a strong conceptual understanding in primary school pupils rather than focusing purely on procedural knowledge. One of his core arguments is that maths should be taught in a way that builds deep understanding through careful attention to structure and connections between concepts.

Haylock's work on the structure of maths is particularly significant. He explains that arithmetic operations, such as addition, subtraction, multiplication and division, are not just isolated processes but are connected through overarching mathematical structures. Teachers who understand these structures can guide their pupils more effectively by helping them recognise patterns and relationships between concepts.

John Sweller and cognitive load theory

Another major strand of research that has influenced maths teaching is cognitive load theory (CLT), developed by John Sweller in the 1980s. CLT posits that working memory has a limited capacity, and when it is overloaded with too much information at once, learning becomes less effective. In the context of maths education, this theory has led to the idea that teaching should be structured to minimise cognitive overload. Sweller's work suggests that using well-organised models and representations, such as the concrete, pictorial, abstract (CPA) framework, can help manage cognitive load by breaking down complex problems into manageable chunks.

Teachers are encouraged to introduce new concepts gradually, building on prior knowledge and using visual aids or manipulatives to reduce the strain on working memory. This approach helps pupils to process information more efficiently, deepening their understanding and enabling them to tackle more complex problems as their skills develop.

Daniel Willingham and working memory

Daniel Willingham, a cognitive psychologist, has written about the role of working memory in learning, particularly in relation to how pupils process and retain information (2009). One of his key contributions is his explanation of the limitations of working memory and how it impacts learning. Willingham suggests that working memory is like a 'bottleneck' in the brain's cognitive processing system. It has limited capacity, meaning it can only hold a small amount of information at any given time. He emphasises that when too much information is loaded into working memory, it can easily become overwhelmed, leading to cognitive overload and hindering learning.

One of his central points is that repeated practice helps transfer information from working memory into long-term memory, where it can be stored and recalled more easily. This process, known as 'automating' knowledge, reduces the strain on working memory over time, as pupils no longer need to actively process information that has been well-learned.

In his book *Why Don't Students Like School?* (2009), Willingham explains that background knowledge plays a crucial role in reducing cognitive load. When pupils have a strong foundation of knowledge in a particular subject, they can more easily make sense of new information, because the relevant prior knowledge is stored in long-term memory and can be accessed without overloading working memory.

Jerome Bruner and the enactive, iconic and symbolic representations

Another key theoretical contribution comes from Jerome Bruner, whose three modes of representation – enactive, iconic and symbolic – have deeply influenced the way maths is taught (1960). These representations describe how knowledge is constructed and stored in the brain at different stages of learning. According to Bruner, learning progresses from the enactive (action-based) stage, where pupils physically manipulate objects to explore mathematical concepts; to the iconic stage, where visual representations like pictures or diagrams help pupils make connections; and finally, to the symbolic stage, where abstract mathematical symbols and notations are used.

Rosenshine and the principles of instruction

Rosenshine's Principles of Instruction (2012) are a set of research-informed teaching strategies developed by educational psychologist Barak Rosenshine. Drawing on evidence from cognitive science, classroom observations, and effective teaching practices, these principles provide a practical framework for high-quality instruction. They are widely used across subjects to support clarity, retention and effective learning. Here are the ten principles (paraphrased from Rosenshine):

- Begin by activating prior knowledge so pupils are ready to learn.
- Break new learning into small, manageable chunks.
- Use purposeful questioning to check in with every learner.
- Make thinking visible through clear modelling.
- Guide pupils through early practice before releasing responsibility.
- Continuously check for understanding and address misconceptions.
- Aim for a high success rate to build confidence and momentum.
- Use scaffolds to support pupils with more challenging content.
- Provide structured opportunities for independent practice.
- Revisit learning regularly to strengthen long-term memory.

Case study: embedding evidence-informed practice in maths teaching and learning

At a one-form-entry school, newly appointed maths subject lead Malia quickly identifies an issue: inconsistent teaching approaches across classrooms. Malia's deputy head works alongside her on book looks, lesson drop-ins, and informal staff conversations. During this time, it becomes clear that while all teachers are committed, they vary significantly in their approaches. Some lessons prioritise speed and procedural fluency, while others focus on rich tasks with little structure, and the use of manipulatives or reasoning prompts is sporadic.

Rather than jumping into a new scheme or launching multiple initiatives, Malia decides to focus on alignment: helping teachers work from a shared, evidence-informed understanding of effective maths teaching.

To guide her thinking, Malia begins by reading the EEF's *Improving Mathematics in Key Stages 2 and 3* report (Henderson et al., 2022), identifying one key theme to work on: enabling pupils to develop a rich network of mathematical knowledge through explicit teaching and modelling.

She remembers reading about Rosenshine's Principles of Instruction (2012) in a previous PD session, so she revisits these too. Knowing her time is limited, Malia:

- listens to education podcasts (Thinking Deeply about Primary Education and Tips for Teachers) on her commute
- sets aside 30 minutes of her subject leadership time each week to read, highlight and summarise relevant sections of the EEF report and Rosenshine's principles
- keeps an informal research journal where she notes implications for her school's context.

With a clearer understanding of what high-quality maths teaching could look like, Malia creates a short, accessible staff training session called *What Does Effective Maths Teaching Look Like at Hawthorn Primary?*. It includes:

- a summary of the research base
- agreed features of a typical maths lesson (e.g. worked examples, guided practice, independent practice)
- flexibility for teacher autonomy, with clear shared expectations.

To support staff engagement:

- Malia leads half-termly PD sessions focusing on live modelling and crafting explanations.
- She uses lesson clips, worked examples and modelling during staff meetings to make the theory more concrete for her colleagues.
- Teachers are asked to trial one strategy at a time and reflect on this during ringfenced time in PD sessions.

Malia avoids making assumptions about impact. Instead, she:

- conducts joint learning walks with other leaders in the school, focusing on the impact of teacher explanations and modelling
- collects staff feedback via short online forms after PD sessions
- organises peer drop-ins, where teachers could observe a colleague trying out a strategy.

By the end of the academic year, key gains are visible:

- Teachers are increasingly using consistent and effective modelling strategies.
- Teachers report feeling more confident and 'clearer on what good maths teaching looks like'.

Malia and her senior leaders don't feel they can see a clear or direct impact on pupil outcomes at this early stage, but they do note that pupils anecdotally report feeling more confident in lessons due to the structured modelling from their teachers. Next, Malia plans to:

1. embed core practices into the induction of new staff
2. develop subject knowledge clinics focused on specific topics (e.g. fractions, proportional reasoning) to give more focused support.

Example PD session: building a research-informed culture

Here is an example of what a PD session on building a research-informed culture could look like.

TIMING SUGGESTION	SESSION GUIDANCE
5 mins	• Briefly introduce the theme of the session 'Why are we talking about research?' • Share anonymised examples of inconsistent practice and the potential impact of allowing these inconsistencies to continue long-term.
5 mins	• Introduce the EEF *Improving Mathematics in KS2 and KS3* report (Henderson et al., 2022). • Depending on how much your school has engaged with the EEF before, you may need to explain that the Education Endowment Foundation is an independent charity looking to improve the educational experience and outcomes of the poorest pupils in English schools. They produce guidance reports to support schools with their school improvement and teaching and learning.

TIMING SUGGESTION	SESSION GUIDANCE

20 mins	• Depending on group size, split the staff into four or eight groups outside of usual teaching teams or phases to get breadth across the school.
	• If in eight groups, give each group one recommendation to read. If in four groups, give each group two to read.
	• Ask them to look at the following things:
	  • What is the recommendation?
	  • How does this relate to current practice in your school?
	  • What is one thing we could take from the recommendation?

20 mins	• Give each group time to share what they read. • Give groups time to discuss what they have heard after each recommendation. • Write down key themes and threads coming out of the conversations.
5 mins	• Wrap up the session by explaining that this is the first in a series of PD sessions to build a research-informed culture. • Give the staff time to consider what new nugget of knowledge they will take away from the session.
Post-session	• Send out the EEF report and put the recommendations poster up in communal areas, e.g. PPA room and staffroom.

This professional development session is a nice way to kickstart a school's journey into becoming more research-informed. Going forward, you can focus on one piece of research as a group and look at its practical application, so staff can take away one thing to implement in their practice.

Questions for reflection

- How can I ensure that I'm critically evaluating research rather than accepting it?
- Do I actively seek out research that challenges my current beliefs or teaching practices?
- How can I balance research findings with the lived experiences of the teachers and pupils in our classrooms?
- What steps can I take to implement research-based strategies gradually and assess their impact before scaling them up?

- How am I fostering a research-informed school culture, and how can I involve all staff in this process?

Explore further

- *Why Don't Students Like School?* (2009) by Daniel Willingham
- *Mathematics Explained for Primary Teachers* (2024) by Derek Haylock
- The EEF's Teaching and Learning Toolkit: https://educationendowmentfoundation.org.uk/education-evidence/teaching-learning-toolkit
- The collection of research papers and articles on Craig Barton's website 'Mr Barton's Maths', available at: https://www.mrbartonmaths.com/research/

Chapter summary

- As a maths leader, engaging with educational research is essential for making informed decisions to improve teaching and learning.
- Not all research is equal, and it's important to critically evaluate the quality and relevance of research before adopting it.
- It's easy to seek out research that supports your pre-existing beliefs. To foster professional growth, engage with research that challenges your assumptions.
- Foster a research-informed culture by sharing findings and encouraging discussion and PD among teachers.
- Research from Haylock and Bruner emphasises the importance of building deep conceptual understanding through structured teaching that connects representations, supports progression and develops secure mathematical thinking.
- Sweller's work on Cognitive Load Theory and Willingham's work on memory highlight the need for carefully sequenced instruction, scaffolding and repeated practice to manage working memory and support long-term learning in maths.

3 School culture and attitudes

We often see negative attitudes in primary maths. Some pupils (and adults) hold a fixed mindset about maths. They view it as a subject that is either easy or difficult, or think that you are either a 'maths person' or not a 'maths person', rather than seeing maths as a subject where effort and persistence lead to success. As a maths leader, your role is crucial in setting a positive tone and reframing these negative views. This chapter will look at the impact a positive maths culture can have, raising the profile of maths within your school and how to engage parents and carers in their children's maths education.

The importance of a positive maths culture

Culture underpins every aspect of school life, influencing how teachers teach and how pupils learn. In primary maths, the culture within a school or classroom can enhance or hinder pupil engagement, confidence and achievement. When we consider the culture of maths in primary schools, this includes attitudes, beliefs, norms and practices surrounding the subject. It can shape how pupils perceive their own abilities and potential. A positive maths culture is one where pupils feel comfortable making mistakes and trying things out, where uncertainty and struggle are normal, by celebrating mathematical thinking, encouraging collaboration and valuing every pupil's contribution (Hattie, 2012).

'School must be a place of relentless positivity when it comes to maths. It is beautiful, it is useful, it is important.' (Garry, 2020, p. 139). Being able to set the culture of maths in your school might feel like a lot of pressure but enjoy it! You can set the tone through your actions, attitudes and the environment you create within your school.

Fostering positive attitudes

Building a culture of positivity around maths in a primary school isn't just about raising attainment – it's about creating an environment where everyone feels motivated and prepared to succeed and sees maths as an interesting, achievable and purposeful subject. Here are some guiding principles to help you lead this cultural shift.

Put teachers first

If you want pupils to feel positive about maths, then we need the teachers to feel positive too. Teachers are the gatekeepers to a pupil's mathematical journey. If they approach maths with confidence and enthusiasm, their pupils are more likely to do the same. However, not every teacher comes equipped with a love for numbers. Some carry negative experiences from their own schooling, which can influence their teaching despite their best efforts to leave it all behind.

As a subject leader, your role is to empower teachers to overcome these barriers. Start by creating a culture of professional trust where teachers feel safe to share their uncertainties about teaching maths with you. Ensure there is a system in place for teachers to work with you on developing their subject knowledge (including pedagogical content knowledge) through coaching, team teaching and peer observations. Hopefully, you will be given some PD sessions to plan and deliver over the course of the year. With multiple school improvement priorities, these sessions are like gold dust as other subject leaders will also want to focus on their subject's needs. When you do have time for these sessions, plan training that is rooted in research and relevant for their practice. Encourage reflective practice, where teachers can share what went well and what could be improved without fear of judgement. Provide resources and model lessons that showcase effective strategies for teaching maths.

Above all, listen to your teachers. Find out what they need to feel more confident and supported in their maths teaching. By putting them first, you're creating a ripple effect of positivity that will reach every pupil in their classroom.

Case study: introducing bar modelling to staff

When Sarah becomes maths lead at her primary school, she quickly realises that problem solving is an area in which both pupils and teachers lack confidence. Discussions with staff reveal that many teachers feel uncomfortable teaching multi-step word problems, often resorting to telling pupils which operation to use rather than developing their reasoning skills. Sarah knows that bar modelling (a visual representation that uses bars to model quantities and relationships) could be a powerful tool to bridge this gap, but she also knows that introducing it successfully would require careful planning and staff buy-in.

Before introducing bar modelling, Sarah spends time observing lessons and talking to teachers about their concerns. She finds that, while some teachers have heard of bar modelling, most aren't sure how to use it effectively. Some believe it is too complex for younger pupils, while others see it as just another method to teach rather than a way to deepen understanding.

To address these misconceptions, Sarah decides that teacher training has to be hands-on. Rather than overwhelming staff with theory, she wants them to experience bar modelling in the same way pupils would.

Sarah runs a staff meeting focused on bar modelling, beginning with a simple question: 'If a pupil doesn't know whether to add or subtract in a word problem, how do you help them?'

The responses are mixed. Some teachers speak about key words like 'altogether' and 'left', while others admit they simply tell pupils which operation to use. Sarah then introduces bar models by demonstrating how they visualise relationships between numbers, rather than relying on key words, which can be misleading.

To build confidence, she asks teachers to work in small groups, solving problems using bar models. Starting with basic part-whole relationships before progressing to comparison models, she makes sure that teachers see how bar modelling can be introduced progressively across year groups.

Rather than leaving teachers to implement bar modelling alone, Sarah offers ongoing support by creating quick at-a-glance guides for teachers to refer to when planning and teaching, and feeding back findings from learning walks. Gradually, teachers gain confidence and begin to see the impact of bar modelling on pupils' reasoning skills.

To ensure bar modelling becomes embedded in the school's practice, Sarah works with colleagues to:

- include bar models in the school's calculation policy, ensuring consistency across year groups
- make bar models a key feature of problem-solving lessons, not just an 'extra' strategy
- share success stories, using staff meetings to celebrate examples of pupil progress.

Raising the profile of maths around school

For maths to be celebrated, it needs to be visible. There has been a huge focus on reading for pleasure in the last decade, but what about maths? Raising the profile of maths in your school means embedding it into the fabric of daily life so that it's seen as much more than just a subject on the timetable.

Create a buzz around maths by including a maths award in your weekly celebration assembly such as the Maths Star of the Week, or the Mathematical Thinker of the Week. This needn't be about 100% scores and attainment though. This is to shine a light on those pupils who are working hard, whether they have previously worked above or below age expectation. Reward perseverance, positivity and effort. While these sorts of awards can seem tokenistic, sometimes we need to draw attention to things for the importance of it to really click for our pupils.

You could also organise whole-school events such as Maths Week England and NSPCC Number Day. Opportunities like this can show off the enjoyment of maths which links to the awe and wonder aspects of the National Curriculum in England (DfE, 2013). Like we often do with British Science Week and World Book Day, giving over a tiny part of our timetable in the year to something 'maths-y' because it's fun and interesting is one way to raise the profile and get pupils (and parents and carers!) talking about maths.

Engage the wider school community by sharing maths successes in newsletters, assemblies, and on social media. Highlighting the joy and relevance of maths in everyday life can help pupils see its importance beyond the classroom.

Here is an example of how to include maths successes in newsletters:

Marvellous Maths at Poppy Parade Primary

We've had a fantastic week of maths and are so proud of the progress, perseverance, and positivity shown across the school. Here's a round-up of some brilliant achievements we're celebrating this week.

Maths Passport Champions
We are delighted to announce the children who have achieved their next Maths Passport level. This means they've mastered the key fluency objectives of their current passport and are ready for the next challenge:

England	**Europe**
Gigi	Josiah
Harriet	Devu
Marco	Oscar
Wales	Aimee
Rupert	**Africa**
Nell	Kelleigh
Arlo	**North America**
Ireland	George
Bobby	Jimi
Jasper	Flynn
Kirsteen	**Pangea**
Luella	Penny

Remember you can come to passport control on Thursdays to get tested!

Times Table Rock Stars Superstars!
A huge congratulations to the following children who have earned the certificate for most improved accuracy in the last week:

Year 2 – Mia
Year 3 – Dylan
Year 4 – Sindi
Year 5 – Kate
Year 6 – Alfie

Keep rocking those times tables – every second counts!

Deep Thinkers of the Week
A special shout-out to these children who have demonstrated deep mathematical thinking this week:
Year 2 – Ava for trying different strategies until she found the most efficient one.
Year 4 – Joseph for making connections between fractions and decimals.
Year 6 – Emily for exploring algebraic patterns and explaining her findings.

Figure 3.1 Example newsletter sharing pupils' success in maths

Positive framing

Whether you're working with pupils, teachers or parents and carers, approach every conversation about maths with positivity. This doesn't mean glossing over challenges but framing them as learning opportunities and goals. Positive framing is an idea often used in relation to behaviour management but it applies to instructional strategies too. Consider the language you use (and therefore model) to pupils and colleagues. What message are we sending with our words?

Here are some examples of how we can flip the narrative and frame our language more positively. It's not about lying and telling pupils they're doing well when they've got everything wrong, but we need to come from a positive place where possible.

In practice: positive framing phrases

INSTEAD OF...	TRY...
'You should know this by now.'	'This links to something we've done before. Let's revisit that before we move on.'
'You did this in Year 1!'	'This builds on what you learned in Year 1, so let's connect it to today's learning.'

'You've forgotten to exchange the ten again.'	'Remind me of the steps we need to take. Let's check if we've used them here. What should it look like?'
'Mrs Brown, Monique hasn't got this at all. Can you take her outside please?'	'Mrs Brown, Monique has understood X and Y so far. I think revisiting Z will help to secure it all. Can she show you what she's got so far please?'

The importance of parental and community engagement

Parental and community engagement can be an important part of shaping a positive culture around maths in primary schools. When parents and carers are involved in their child's education, they are better equipped to support learning at home, and pupils benefit from consistent messages about the value of maths. If they express enthusiasm and confidence, pupils are more likely to approach the subject positively. Conversely, if parents and carers convey doubt or anxiety about maths, pupils may internalise these feelings, potentially affecting their motivation and performance. Community engagement extends this influence, showing pupils that maths is relevant beyond the classroom. Highlighting real-world applications and the importance of mathematical thinking in various professions can inspire a deeper appreciation for the subject.

How to get parents and carers on board

When it comes to engaging parents and carers, you need to meet them where they are. It's no good putting on a workshop that you think they need when you don't understand their starting point or haven't yet found the sort of events they are likely to engage with. You can use existing structures such as the Parent Teacher Association (PTA), parent and carer coffee mornings or a family forum to communicate with the parents and carers who already engage with the school first. Acknowledge that the maths curriculum will have changed since they were in primary school and that the way we teach maths has changed over time, so it is understandable to feel confused by it. Is it that they have heard about 'bar modelling' but haven't a clue what it is? Are they using different or outdated vocabulary — for example, borrowing and carrying? If you think they need a starting point, then you could suggest three or four ideas for family workshops to see which one piques their interest most. Some parents and carers will be more than happy to give you ideas. Once you have a plan of action for family workshop content, consider how to reach the most parents and carers. Do you move things online so that childcare isn't a barrier or send out pre-recorded videos that families can access when it suits them? Do you offer more than one session, e.g. 9.00 am after drop off, 2.00 pm before pick-up or 6.00 pm after work? You will know your community best, so it's worth considering your own context and what will work best for the parents and carers of your pupils.

Communication is everything when it comes to culture. Think about how you communicate with parents and carers in your school. As a profession, we've come on leaps and bounds with phonics and getting families clued up on early reading, so talk to your colleagues who lead English and teach phonics to see how they have communicated messages effectively. Do you have a communication app, newsletters or social media? How can you keep maths within the communication strategy for your school? Could you highlight upcoming topics in different year groups, suggest mathematically-rich activities for home, or celebrate maths successes from across the school? Could you share picture books that link to maths and offer talking points and questions to ask when reading them at home? Here is a list to get you started:

- *One is a Snail, Ten is a Crab* by April Pulley Sayre and Jeff Sayre, 2003
- *How Many Jelly Beans?* by Andrea Menotti, 2012
- *How Big is a Million?* by Anna Milbourne, 2007
- *One Hundred Hungry Ants* by Elinor J. Pinczes, 1993
- *How Many Legs?* by Kes Gray, 2015
- *Equal Shmequal* by Virginia L Kroll, 2005
- *A Place For Zero* by Angeline Lopresti, 1995
- *Sir Cumference and All the King's Tens* by Cindy Neuschwander, 2009

Tackling the 'not a maths person' mentality

One of the most common barriers to parental and pupil engagement is the belief that some people 'just don't have a maths brain' and therefore can't succeed in maths. This is an educational myth with no empirical evidence behind it. It's vital to remember that this attitude often stems from the families' own negative experiences of maths at school. We want to challenge this as maths leaders and teachers, but we also don't want to alienate parents and carers by coming on too strong! We should aim to model the idea that anyone can achieve and succeed in maths with effective teaching and lots of practice. As leaders, we can encourage parents and carers to model this at home too, so we are on the same team rather than battling with them.

To make maths relatable and enjoyable, you can set everyday tasks as optional home learning such as budgeting, cooking and planning a holiday. These tasks show pupils how maths applies to real life, bridging the gap between the classroom and the world beyond. For example, asking pupils to help plan a weekly food shop within a specific budget can develop skills in addition, subtraction and estimation, while also teaching financial responsibility. Cooking offers opportunities to explore measurement, fractions and multiplication through scaling recipes, weighing ingredients and converting units. Finally, planning a holiday or a day out provides a rich, multi-step activity where pupils can practise time calculations, map reading and comparing costs. Encourage families to involve children in discussions about decisions, such as finding the best deals or understanding value for money, to make the experience interactive and meaningful.

If you do set maths homework in your school, consider putting on an optional challenge for families to work on together; the NRICH site has some excellent problems that can be solved at home.

Reward effort and process over accuracy by offering team or house points for trying it out rather than getting it right. Email the homework to parents and carers in advance so that they know what is coming home with the pupils, and offer them suggested questions or starting points along with the answers for when they want to double check. Without this, we run the risk of making them feel inadequate for not just 'getting it'. Plus, if the pupils see their families engaging with a maths problem positively, they are more likely to engage positively too.

Reaching out to the wider community

'But why do I even need to know this?' is a classic line in maths lessons. Beyond the basics of arithmetic, many pupils (and sometimes their families) can't see the use of a lot of what we teach in primary school maths. Reach out to the wider community to showcase how maths can be used in a range of professions. Start with local businesses and professionals, some of whom might be parents/carers or relatives of your pupils. Invite a range of people in for a maths careers afternoon where they can speak and demonstrate how they use maths in their jobs. It isn't just accountants and teachers who use maths – think about builders, engineers, chefs, retailers, hairdressers and more. You could also contact secondary schools, colleges and universities who could put on enrichment sessions or provide resources for maths events and workshops that will engage the pupils in maths activities. This will support your role by opening up the minds of the pupils and their families about the importance (and the joy!) of maths. You could feature a diverse range of people from pupils to professionals in the community in assemblies, and regular communications to parents and carers in newsletters or social media.

Case study: engaging parents and carers in a 'difficult to reach' community

James is the maths leader at a coastal, one-form-entry primary school. He knows that parental engagement in maths is low. Parents and carers have the opinion that they are either 'maths people' or they aren't, and more than often it is that they aren't. Homework is rarely completed, attendance at family workshops is poor and many parents and carers openly admit to disliking maths themselves. James wants to break the cycle by helping families feel more confident in supporting their children's learning, but he knows that simply running another 'How We Teach Maths' evening won't work.

Rather than assuming he knows why families aren't engaging, James starts by listening. He sets up informal chats at school drop-off, attends a parent and carer coffee morning and speaks to staff who live in the community. Several key issues emerge:

- Parents and carers feel embarrassed about their own maths skills and don't want to feel 'tested' in workshops.
- They don't understand modern methods, especially for arithmetic, and worry about confusing their children.
- Workshops are inconvenient: many parents and carers have younger children to look after or work shifts.

James changes the school's approach:

- Short, informal maths drop-ins in the school hall with him and a senior leader just before pick-up time encourage parents and carers to watch quick maths demos when they are already going to be on site.
- Video tutorials on a parental communication app provide short, friendly explanations of key methods that parents and carers can watch in their own time.
- Family Maths Challenges include simple, practical activities that parents and carers can do with their children at home, like cooking or budgeting.

One of the biggest successes is a 'Maths and Biscuits' morning, in which families join their children for a relaxed, non-intimidating maths session. Parents and carers aren't asked to solve problems themselves: instead, teachers model how they teach maths, giving families confidence in how to support their children.

James realises that one-off workshops won't change attitudes overnight. He focuses on building trust through regular updates in newsletters and on social media, celebrating small successes and encouraging teachers to share maths moments at parents' evenings, rather than just discussing progress.

Gradually, attitudes begin to shift. Attendance at drop-in sessions starts to grow, and families start asking more questions about how to help at home. While these are signs of progress, James knows there is still a long way to go. Not all parents and carers are engaged, and many still lack confidence. Rather than continuing to add more initiatives, James feels it is important to let these ones embed and re-evaluate in two terms' time by sending out a parent survey on maths.

Example PD session: changing attitudes

Here is an example of what a PD session on changing attitudes could look like.

TIMING SUGGESTION	SESSION GUIDANCE
10 mins	• Welcome the staff and share the session objectives. You will be focusing on recognising how fixed mindsets impact pupil (and adult) attitudes to maths. • Introduce the myth that some people aren't maths people or just aren't good at maths. • Explain how beliefs shape effort, resilience and achievement in maths.
10 mins	• Invite teachers to reflect on their current practice. How do they talk to pupils? How do pupils talk about maths? • Prompt them with 'I have heard a pupil say...' or 'When a child says they can't do it, I usually respond by...' • Use think, pair, share so the staff have time to reflect on their practice and classroom culture before sharing with their partner and then the whole group.
15 mins	• Introduce the concept of positive framing. • Share the examples from earlier in this chapter. You could also add in some more examples based on what people have shared or what you have heard in learning walks. • Give teachers three to five 'fixed mindset' phrases on strips of paper, e.g. 'You've always struggled with your times tables.' Ask them to rewrite each one using positive framing. • Share these with the rest of the group and observe how people's positively framed versions compare. • Discuss how a simple shift in language could impact attitudes and promote confidence.

15 mins	• Explore some classroom strategies to tackle the 'not a maths person' mentality:
	    • Modelling a positive attitude to errors.
	    • Celebrating effort over correctness.
	    • Using accessible challenges so everyone can access them.
	• Share a case study or a video clip (you could film yourself in class) and discuss the strategy used, the impact of it and how to make it more effective.

5 mins	• Invite teachers to commit to one change that they will try over the next week. You could provide a frame such as: What will I try? When will I try it? How will I know if it's having an impact?
5 mins	• Summarise the key points. • Share any follow-up resources that have come up during the lesson. • Invite ongoing discussion by letting them know you'll revisit the topic in a future PD session.

Questions for reflection

- How does our school's culture currently support or hinder positive attitudes towards maths?
- What steps can we take to identify and address the needs of teachers in our school, regarding their confidence and competence in teaching maths?
- What strategies could we implement to engage parents more effectively in supporting their children's learning and attitudes toward maths?

Explore further

- *Engaging Parents* (2016) by Naomi Eisenstadt
- Headteacher Update's *Six steps for a positive mindset in the maths classroom* by Alexandra Riley: https://www.headteacher-update.com/content/best-practice/six-steps-for-a-positive-mindset-in-the-maths-classroom/
- Training & Technical Assistance Center's Promoting a math-positive school culture (2022): https://ttac.odu.edu/product/promoting-a-math-positive-school-culture/

Chapter summary

- A positive maths culture where pupils feel comfortable making mistakes and trying things out can be forged by celebrating mathematical thinking, encouraging collaboration and valuing every pupil's contribution.
- As a maths leader, promoting a growth mindset and reframing negative attitudes about maths is central to fostering confidence and resilience in learners.
- Supporting teachers with PD, coaching and collaborative practices is key to fostering a positive attitude towards maths.
- Embedding maths into school life, organising events and celebrating successes can raise its profile and build enthusiasm.
- Collaboration with parents and community members helps to demystify maths, model positive attitudes and highlight its real-world relevance.

4 Progression and curriculum structure

A well-structured curriculum is the key to effective maths teaching for pupils from EYFS to the end of Key Stage 2 (KS2) and beyond. In this chapter, we will explore the principles of curriculum design and the importance of coherence, ensuring concepts build logically and meaningfully over time. We will consider how progression should be carefully mapped, enabling pupils to develop secure foundations in early maths that support more complex problem solving and reasoning in later stages.

Curriculum design

Understanding curriculum coherence is a fundamental aspect of leading a subject. Ensuring that what is taught is logically sequenced, developmentally appropriate and aligned with clear goals for learning is an important part of your role. In maths, where knowledge is often hierarchical and builds progressively, a coherent curriculum plays a pivotal role in ensuring that pupils develop both fluency and a deep understanding of concepts over time.

Maths as a hierarchical subject

Maths is widely recognised as a hierarchical subject meaning that new concepts often depend on the mastery of previous knowledge (Schmidt et al., 2005). For example, pupils must understand place value before tackling addition and subtraction, and they must have a solid grasp of multiplication to access fractions or algebra. This interconnected nature requires a curriculum that has been carefully planned so that pupils are exposed to concepts in a logical order. When this level of coherence is achieved, pupils are less likely to experience gaps in understanding that can hinder future learning. Instead, they build a secure foundation of knowledge that supports more advanced thinking. The National Curriculum for England (DfE, 2013) is the best place to start if you need to know how to order specific knowledge and concepts.

Coherence in the maths curriculum

In the National Curriculum in England (DfE, 2013), there are big concepts that act as umbrella terms for the concepts that sit within them:

- number – number and place value
- number – addition and subtraction
- number – multiplication and division
- number – fractions including decimals and percentages
- measurement
- geometry – properties of shapes
- geometry – position and direction
- statistics
- ratio and proportion
- algebra.

Let's look at just one of these to see how the concepts progress over time.

STAGE	**STEPS FOR PROGRESSION** (Adapted from the National Curriculum for Mathematics (DfE, 2014))
EYFS	• Explore and represent patterns within numbers up to 10, including evens and odds, double facts and how quantities can be distributed equally.
YEAR 1	• Recognise, find and name a half as 1 of 2 equal parts of an object, shape or quantity. • Recognise, find and name a quarter as 1 of 4 equal parts of an object, shape or quantity.
YEAR 2	• Recognise, find, name and write fractions $\frac{1}{3}$, $\frac{1}{4}$, $\frac{2}{4}$ and $\frac{3}{4}$ of a length, shape, set of objects or quantity. • Write simple fractions [for example, in the statement $\frac{1}{2}$ of 6 = 3]. • Recognise the equivalence of $\frac{2}{4}$ and $\frac{1}{2}$.
YEAR 3	• Count up and down in tenths. • Recognise that tenths arise from dividing an object into 10 equal parts and in dividing one-digit numbers or quantities by 10. • Recognise, find and write fractions of a discrete set of objects: unit fractions and non-unit fractions with small denominators.

STAGE	**STEPS FOR PROGRESSION** (Adapted from the National Curriculum for Mathematics (DfE, 2014))
	• Recognise and show, using diagrams, equivalent fractions with small denominators. • Add and subtract fractions with the same denominator within one whole [for example, $\frac{5}{7}+\frac{1}{7}=\frac{6}{7}$]. • Compare and order unit fractions, and fractions with the same denominators. • Solve problems that involve all of the above.
YEAR 4	• Recognise and show, using diagrams, families of common equivalent fractions. • Count up and down in hundredths. • Recognise that hundredths arise when dividing an object by 100 and dividing tenths by 10. • Solve problems involving increasingly hard fractions to calculate quantities, and fractions to divide quantities, including non-unit fractions, where the answer is a whole number. • Add and subtract fractions with the same denominator. • Recognise and write decimal equivalents of any number of tenths or hundreds. • Recognise and write decimal equivalents to $\frac{1}{4}$, $\frac{1}{2}$ and $\frac{3}{4}$. • Find the effect of dividing a one- or two-digit number by 10 and 100, identifying the values of the digits in the answer as ones, tenths and hundredths. • Round decimals with 1 decimal place to the nearest whole number. • Compare numbers with the same number of decimal places, up to 2 decimal places. • Solve simple measure and money problems involving fractions and decimals to 2 decimal places.
YEAR 5	• Compare and order fractions whose denominators are all multiples of the same number. • Identify, name and write equivalent fractions of a given fraction represented visually, including tenths and hundredths. • Recognise mixed numbers and improper fractions and convert from one form to the other. • Write mathematical statements > 1 as mixed numbers [for example, $\frac{2}{5}+\frac{4}{5}=\frac{6}{5}=1\frac{1}{5}$]. • Add and subtract fractions with the same denominator, and denominators that are multiples of the same number. • Multiply proper fractions and mixed numbers by whole numbers, supported by materials and diagrams. • Read and write decimal numbers as fractions [for example, $0.71 = \frac{71}{100}$].

STAGE	STEPS FOR PROGRESSION (Adapted from the National Curriculum for Mathematics (DfE, 2014))
	• Recognise and use thousandths and relate them to tenths, hundredths and decimal equivalents. • Round decimals with 2 decimal places to the nearest whole number and to 1 decimal place. • Read, write, order and compare numbers with up to 3 decimal places. • Solve problems involving numbers up to 3 decimal places. • Recognise the per cent symbol (%) and understand that per cent relates to 'number of parts per 100'. • Write percentages as fractions with denominator 100, and as decimal fractions. • Solve problems that require knowing percentage and decimal equivalents of $\frac{1}{2}$, $\frac{1}{4}$, $\frac{1}{5}$, $\frac{2}{5}$ and $\frac{4}{5}$, and fractions with a denominator of a multiple of 10 or 25.
YEAR 6	• Use common factors to simplify fractions. • Use common multiples to express fractions in the same denomination. • Compare and order fractions, including fractions > 1. • Add and subtract fractions with different denominators and mixed numbers, using the concept of equivalent fractions. • Multiply simple pairs of proper fractions, writing the answers in their simplest forms [for example, $\frac{1}{4} \times \frac{1}{2} = \frac{1}{8}$]. • Divide proper fractions by whole numbers [for example, $\frac{1}{3} \div 2 = \frac{1}{6}$]. • Associate a fraction with division and calculate decimal fraction equivalents [for example, 0.375] for a simple fraction [for example, $\frac{3}{8}$]. • Identify the value of each digit in numbers given to 3 decimal places. • Multiply and divide numbers by 10, 100 and 1,000 giving answers up to 3 decimal places. • Multiply one-digit numbers with up to 2 decimal places by whole numbers. • Use written division methods in cases where the answer has up to 2 decimal places. • Solve problems that require answers to be rounded to specified degrees of accuracy. • Recall and use equivalences between simple fractions, decimals and percentages, including in different contexts.

Looking at a long list of objectives to see how fractions, decimals and percentages progresses over time is quite an overwhelming task. For big areas within the National Curriculum in England, it might be better to organise the objectives into strands so that there are mini progression threads within one big area.

For fractions, you could organise the objectives into the following strands:

- recognising, identifying and representing fractions
- equivalence
- comparing and ordering
- adding and subtracting
- multiplying and dividing
- rounding
- problem solving.

There is no 'right' way to organise your curriculum and you absolutely don't have to break each big area down into strands. The aim of doing this is to chunk content into smaller progression threads that build logically across year groups. This isn't about inventing new content but making the existing objectives more usable for planning, teaching and assessment.

Start by printing out or highlighting the national curriculum objectives for Years 1 to 6 and begin sorting them under headings that make sense for your school's approach. Your scheme of work (if you use one) may already organise objectives in this way, which can help guide your structure, but it's important to adapt this to fit your pupils, staff and broader curriculum links. For example, some schools align measures topics with science or geography units to support cross-curricular learning, while others cluster number topics at the start of the year for depth before breadth. What matters most is that your structure supports progression, retrieval and teacher clarity, so it's fine if it looks different from another school's. This process will support teachers in making connections within maths, and in better understanding the journey each strand takes from one year to the next.

The benefits of separating each big curriculum idea into these strands include the following:

- Teachers can see how concepts evolve from the foundational skills to more complex ideas.
- It highlights the hierarchical nature of maths and gives prerequisite knowledge for each strand, preventing gaps from forming.
- Teachers have a clear progression document for each idea in the curriculum, so know what has come before and what is coming next.

- Teachers can use it to adapt their teaching for those pupils who are not working at the expected standard.
- Less experienced teachers can use it as a framework to see the big idea and how it connects and develops over time.
- You can focus your PD time on one strand at a time to look at vocabulary being taught and models and representations being used, in order to streamline strategies and optimise teachers' explanations, therefore maximising pupils' learning.
- Your monitoring of how concepts are taught, learned and retained in your school can be more focused by looking at strands within big ideas, rather than a whole topic like fractions in one go.
- Stakeholders, such as governors and parents and carers, can see how each area within maths is being broken down and taught.

Adopting and adapting schemes of work

In primary maths, it is becoming more and more common to purchase or source an 'off-the-shelf' scheme of work as a foundation for curriculum planning. Pre-designed schemes of work offer many benefits, but there are also drawbacks to consider when implementing one of these schemes in your school. As a subject leader, you may be in the position where you can critically evaluate these schemes and decide on the best fit. Alternatively, you might be taking on maths in a school with a scheme of work that is already established and embedded. If this is the case, you will need to consider how to adapt and continue improving your school's use of the scheme.

Benefits of adopting an 'off-the-shelf' scheme of work

- There should be a well-designed, logical progression built into the scheme, ensuring curriculum coverage across year groups.
- Less confident or less experienced teachers can use them to fill gaps in their own knowledge and understanding.
- With workload at such a high, a bought-in scheme saves time on creating plans and resources from scratch.
- Most English schemes are aligned with the National Curriculum in England (DfE, 2013), ensuring compliance with statutory requirements.

- A shared scheme across a school provides consistency across year groups and classes.
- Subject knowledge can be developed through the use of a scheme of work developed by experts in maths.

Drawbacks of adopting an 'off-the-shelf' scheme of work

- They can sometimes feel prescriptive, leaving teachers without the autonomy to make decisions about task-design and adapting to the needs of their pupils.
- Teachers can become overly reliant on a ready-made scheme which can deskill them as a professional.
- An 'off-the-shelf' scheme may not provide flexibility or relevance for your pupils' needs and experiences.
- Not all schemes are of equal quality. Some lack depth in certain areas, underestimate the need for 'little and often' fluency practice, leave out key models and representations, or neglect opportunities for meaningful variation.

Finding a scheme of work

Choosing a scheme of work is a significant decision that can shape your school's maths curriculum for years to come. To ensure the scheme aligns with your vision and meets the needs of your pupils, a rigorous evaluation process is essential. Ask yourself the following questions about any scheme of work that you are looking at:

- Does it align with the National Curriculum in England or the curriculum that we are using?
- Are concepts sequenced in small steps and revisited over time?
- Does it promote learning and retention?
- Does it align with our school's curriculum vision and goals?
- Is it ambitious enough for our pupils?

Next, look at the pedagogy used in the schemes of work that you are evaluating. Wiliam (2013, p.9) states, 'We cannot really talk about curriculum without talking about pedagogy'. The National Curriculum in England (DfE, 2013) is the intended curriculum, but we need pedagogy for the enacted curriculum – the curriculum that your pupils will experience.

- Does it prioritise conceptual understanding?
- Does it use concrete manipulatives to introduce new content? If not, is this something that me and my colleagues can supplement?
- Are there opportunities for repeated practice?
- What pedagogical values are important in our school and how well aligned is this scheme of work?

Finally, have a look at the resources that come with the scheme of work.

- How resourced do I want our maths curriculum to be for teachers? Am I looking for lesson plans, teaching slides, worksheets and assessments, or detailed medium term plans that the teachers take and turn into lesson materials themselves?

Only you can answer these questions because you know your school's needs. If you are able to pilot a scheme of work in one or two year groups, then take this opportunity so that you can gather input from teachers, observe pupil engagement and outcomes, and use this feedback to make a final decision.

Adapting a scheme of work

Adopting a scheme of work is just the first step. To maximise its impact, you must take ownership of it and embed it within your school's culture. Ensure that you and your staff understand the rationale behind the structure and methods in the scheme of work. Provide PD when introducing the new scheme of work. Don't underestimate how much time you will need for this! One session is not enough. If you are adopting a new scheme of work, give one session over to the technical bits like log-ins, navigating a website and getting to know any physical resources. Then, give another session over to the rationale behind the change, the way the scheme of work has been designed and developed, and how your school intends to use it. Then ideally, you'd have at least one more session on taking the scheme of work and planning from it, designing tasks or supplementing ready-made tasks with appropriate scaffolds or challenges. It can be difficult to get this much time in a busy professional development schedule, but it will be worth it if you can.

It might also be necessary to supplement the scheme of work with additional resources, manipulatives or tasks to enrich learning. Your position on this should be very clear to staff. Some schools emphasise fidelity to one scheme with little flexibility, whereas others will have clear guidelines on what parts are flexible and can be supplemented as long as the quality is the same or better. For example, where some schemes have the same, formulaic approach to task design in each lesson, you may want to adapt the structure to allow for more varied fluency or deeper problem solving.

Another part of adapting a scheme is when thinking about providing additional support or challenge for those pupils working outside of the expected standard. Some schemes of work will provide three-way differentiated tasks, but this isn't considered best practice and may limit what some pupils can achieve. Consider strategies that teachers can use in conjunction with the materials from the scheme of work for adaptive teaching. You might work in a school that already has strategies for scaffolding, such as backwards fading, embedded across the curriculum. Alternatively, you might want to work alongside your teaching and learning lead to implement new strategies.

Case study: adapting a bought-in maths scheme to fit school context

When Priya takes on the role of maths lead at her primary school, the staff are using a well-known 'off-the-shelf' maths scheme. While teachers appreciate the clear sequencing, structured lesson plans and ready-made teaching slides, Priya notices that the scheme isn't always meeting the needs of their pupils. Some topics are covered too briefly, fluency practice is inconsistent and the problem-solving tasks often lack depth. Rather than abandoning the scheme, Priya sets out to make small but meaningful adaptations to ensure it works for their school, their teachers and, most importantly, their pupils.

Priya begins by holding discussions with staff, observing lessons and reviewing pupil outcomes. Key themes emerge:

- The scheme moves too quickly through some complex topics, meaning pupils don't always have time to secure understanding.

- Some teachers feel constrained by the rigid lesson structures.
- There is a gap in retrieval practice, meaning previously taught concepts aren't being revisited systematically.
- Some elements of the scheme work well, such as its clear progression and consistency across year groups.

Rather than making wholesale changes, Priya focuses on small, targeted adaptations that will enhance the scheme's effectiveness while maintaining its structure. She works collaboratively with teachers and her deputy headteacher to slow down the pacing of certain units. They put in place longer timeframes for key concepts like place value, the four operations and fractions; readjust some of the small steps in the units for geometry, statistics and measure; and find solid cross-curricular links through which some of the application can be done. They also update the assessment process by using quick diagnostic checks so that teachers can identify areas where pupils need more time and adjust accordingly.

One issue with the scheme is that fluency tasks are repetitive and don't always build conceptual understanding. Priya introduces:

- a daily fluency session: a 'five a day' arithmetic routine that revisits number bonds, times tables and written calculations from previous weeks
- retrieval questions woven into lessons: retrieval questions written by teachers specifically for their classes, rather than those that the scheme of work suggests.

The scheme also includes problem-solving tasks, but many are formulaic rather than encouraging deep mathematical thinking. Priya works with teachers to introduce:

- low-threshold, high-ceiling problems, which are problems that all pupils can access (low-threshold) while offering opportunities for deepening understanding (high-ceiling), such as this example:

In practice: low-threshold, high-ceiling problem

You have 24 counters.

How many rectangles can you make with 24 counters?

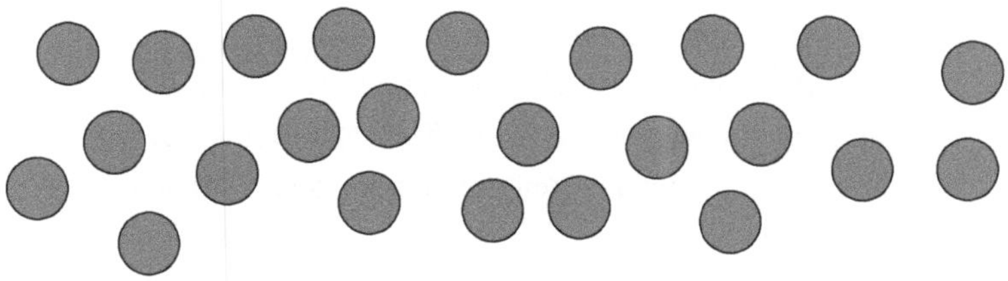

Figure 4.1 24 circular counters

Low-threshold

- All pupils can physically manipulate the counters to create rectangles.
- Everyone can begin to use 'arrays' to describe the rectangles.
- Pupils may begin to notice patterns or multiplication facts.

High-ceiling:

- Pupils can work systematically to find all the possibilities.
- They can explore connections between factors and multiples.
- Pupils could investigate generalisations such as 'Do all even numbers make arrays?'.
- Teachers could prompt pupils to create their own version of this problem.
- Sentence stems for reasoning provide a structured way for pupils to explain their thinking, particularly for those who struggle with verbalising their reasoning, such as 'When we add three numbers, we can add them in any order and the sum will remain the same.'
- A wider range of problem types can supplement the scheme's problem-solving activities with open-ended tasks from NRICH and NCETM.

Priya knows that simply handing out new guidance won't be enough. She takes a gradual, supportive approach by spacing out staff meetings that drip-feed changes over time. With the support of her senior leaders who arrange release time for teams of teachers, she introduces lesson study cycles in which teachers plan, teach and reflect on lessons together.

When Priya conducts another round of evaluative tasks, including drop-ins, pupil voice and staff voice, she finds that there is greater depth in the 'meatier' units on number and that pupils have better retention over time.

Communicating the curriculum

As a subject leader, part of your role requires you to ensure that your colleagues understand the curriculum progression and sequencing. Having a well-written and carefully sequenced curriculum in place will go some way to do this, but you should consider how you communicate the progression and sequencing. Teachers should understand where the pupils have come from so that they can effectively plan for retrieval and then build on this to teach new content. They should also understand what comes next so that they leave the pupils ready and primed for the next year group's content at the end of the year.

Questions for reflection

- How does our current maths curriculum ensure coherence and logical progression?
- How do I ensure all staff understand how key concepts in maths develop over time?
- What criteria would I prioritise when selecting or evaluating a scheme of work, to ensure it aligns with our school's vision and the needs of our pupils?
- How could we adapt an off-the-shelf scheme to address the specific strengths and challenges for our school's pupils and staff?

- What steps can I take to ensure staff are confident in using and adapting a scheme of work? How can we foster collaboration to maximise its impact?

Example PD session: adopting a new scheme of work

Rather than a one-off PD session, consider writing an ongoing plan for how to introduce your staff to a new scheme of work, and to train them on the principles, pedagogy and ways to adapt it.

The following tables are an example of what a PD plan for adopting a new scheme of work could look like.

Preparation

COHORT INVOLVED	TIMING	SESSION GUIDANCE
Leadership team	1 hour	• Meet with senior leaders and familiarise them with the new scheme of work to ensure they understand the scheme's structure, rationale and pedagogical approach.
Subject leader	3 hours	• Arrange log-ins for all staff ahead of the first PD session. • Download relevant documents and save them centrally. • Prepare example materials to give to staff.

Introduction

COHORT INVOLVED	TIMING	SESSION GUIDANCE
Teaching staff	2 hours	• Introduce the new scheme to teaching staff, including TAs if possible. • Run through the rationale behind the scheme, the progression and sequence, pedagogical principles and lesson structures. • Show staff the resources available and explain how they can be used. • Give a demonstration of the lesson structures, resources to use and how you might supplement it. • Direct staff to the materials either online or in a central, cloud-based storage system. Give out log-ins.

Teaching staff	1 hour	• Model planning using the new scheme of work. You could demonstrate how to create an S plan* for a unit of work in one year group, or if this level of thinking is already done in your scheme of work, then you could model how to pull everything together to create the finished lesson materials. • Break into year groups to plan collaboratively using the same model. • Feedback on how it went and discuss strategies for adaptive teaching.

*An S plan is a method of planning a sequence of learning. First, you draw a big S on a sheet of paper and identify the end point or desired outcome. Next, you 'cover the table' with sticky notes of all the small steps, key vocabulary, stem sentences, potential misconceptions, representations and manipulatives. Then, you organise them into the S on your paper in the order they need to be learned. Here is a picture of an S plan.

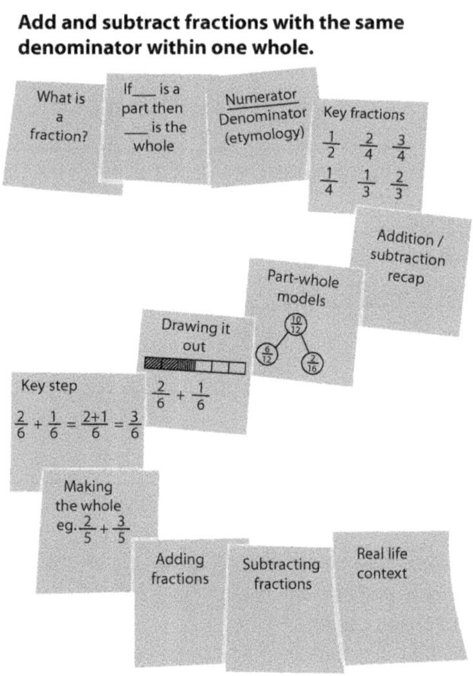

Figure 4.2 An example of an S plan

Classroom trial

COHORT INVOLVED	TIMING	SESSION GUIDANCE
Teaching staff and leadership	Ongoing (Term 1)	• Coach teachers on planning with the new scheme of work. • Conduct drop-ins and coaching on teaching with the new scheme of work. • Set up peer observations within year groups focusing on key elements, such as models and representations, giving explanations or adaptive teaching. • Pull together general successes to share with staff.
Teaching staff	1 hour	• Follow up session after the first term using the new scheme. • Give staff time to share their experiences, successes and challenges. • Revisit key principles and clarify misconceptions. • Share strategies for effective use of the scheme of work.

Ongoing development

COHORT INVOLVED	TIMING	SESSION GUIDANCE
Teaching assistants	1 hour	• Train TAs in formative assessment strategies so that they can support the teachers in checking for understanding. • Model how to use evidence from lessons. For example, using the work in books to pull together same-day interventions, helping to reduce gaps and keep pupils together for the main instruction in class.
Teaching staff	Ongoing (Term 2)	• Join PPA time with all year groups to support them with their maths planning. • Coach them through using the scheme of work and creating lesson materials, supplementing where necessary.
Teaching staff and leadership	Ongoing (Term 3 and beyond)	• Conduct ongoing drop-ins and coaching to enhance teachers' understanding of the new scheme of work.

Explore further

- The chapter 'Curriculum coherence: how best to do it' by Neil Almond in *The ResearchED Guide to The Curriculum* (2020) edited by Clare Sealy
- *Primary Curriculum Design: Planning for Ofsted's Intent, Implementation and Impact* (2026) by Jon Hutchinson
- *Principled Curriculum Design* (2013) by Dylan Wiliam

Chapter summary

- A well-structured and coherent maths curriculum ensures concepts build logically, supporting pupils' mastery of foundational skills and their ability to tackle complex reasoning and problem solving.
- Breaking the curriculum into strands clarifies development, highlights prerequisite knowledge, and aids in planning, monitoring and PD.
- Maths is hierarchical; understanding depends on prior knowledge. A coherent curriculum enables concepts to be revisited and deepened over time.
- Pre-designed schemes offer consistency, support and workload reduction, but require critical evaluation and adaptation to fit school and pupil needs.

5 Fluency

Fluency is crucial to mathematical proficiency, but it is easy to misunderstand or misconstrue fluency as purely fact recall. In this chapter, we will look at the key types of fluency, how to maximise fluency for automaticity and deep understanding and how your role as a maths subject leader requires you to have a secure grasp of where fluency fits into the curriculum.

Understanding fluency in primary maths

Fluency in maths is the ability to work with numbers accurately, efficiently and flexibly.

Working **accurately** means producing correct answers reliably and avoiding errors. Working **efficiently** means choosing methods that are quick and effective for the task at hand. And working **flexibly** means being able to approach problems in different ways, make connections and apply number sense to decide which strategy works best.

Misconceptions about fluency

There are several misconceptions about fluency in primary maths that are borne out of a misunderstanding of how we learn and what fluency looks like. Here are some examples of misconceptions about fluency.

- **'Fluency equals speed.'** Fluency is often associated with answering questions or completing calculations quickly. While speed can be an indicator of fluency and pupils are likely to get faster as their fluency develops, this is just one part of being fluent in maths.
- **'Fluency requires rote learning.'** To do something 'by rote' is to repeat something mechanically, without meaning, until it is memorised. While memorisation of facts will play a part, fluency is grounded in a deep understanding of number and numerical relationships. Repetition alone will not result in true fluency.
- **'Fluency is the same as mastery.'** Mastery of concepts encompasses fluency, reasoning and problem solving. A pupil might be proficient in

procedures but lack the depth of understanding to reason. Fluency alone is not sufficient to demonstrate mastery.

- **'Only high attainers can achieve fluency.'** Mathematical fluency is essential for all pupils, including those with barriers to their learning. It can be achieved with practice over time.
- **'Low-attaining pupils can do only fluency work.'** In contrast to the previous misconception, some may think that a pupil who has previously worked only below expectations should access only fluency practice and not have the opportunity to reason and articulate their thoughts. All pupils can and should have the chance to reason and think mathematically with the right scaffolds and support.
- **'Fluency is only about arithmetic.'** Fluency does not just apply to the four operations. Pupils can be fluent in geometry, measurement and more. We should be aiming for our pupils to achieve a level of fluency in all areas of maths. Arithmetic fluency might be easier to test regularly, but fluency across the curriculum has its place too.
- **'Fluency comes easily.'** Pupils won't always achieve fluency without struggle or difficulty. Struggle, when managed effectively, is a productive part of learning. It helps pupils form connections and deepen their understanding, leading to robust fluency.

Conceptual understanding and procedural knowledge

Fluency requires conceptual understanding and procedural knowledge (NCETM, 2025). Conceptual understanding refers to the deep understanding of the underlying structures involved in a concept or idea. For example, seeing that the problem: 'There are 13 children on the bus. 9 more children get on. How many children are on the bus now?' is an example of augmentation. You start with an amount and increase it rather than having two parts that you bring together. Procedural knowledge is the ability to carry out algorithms accurately and efficiently. For example, being able to use a written method for short multiplication to answer 345 x 8 instead of relying on related facts or partitioning.

In primary maths, we want to strike the right balance of prioritising both conceptual understanding and procedural knowledge. You might think of the conceptual understanding as the 'how and why it works' over the 'what to do' that you get from procedural knowledge. You might think that one needs to be taught before the other, but really, they can be taught in tandem with each other and the content might dictate where you start each time.

Conceptual understanding can lead to greater adaptability when carrying out mathematical procedures, and procedural knowledge can lead to greater efficiency freeing up space to think deeply about the maths at hand. Too much focus on the conceptual understanding can lead to a lack of speed and accuracy when solving calculations, and too much reliance on procedural fluency results in a poor understanding of the underlying structure and therefore *why* and *how* a particular procedure works.

Table 1 on the following pages gives examples of the difference between conceptual understanding and procedural knowledge.

Both the KS1 and KS2 examples in the table demonstrate why we need to teach both the concept and the procedure so that the pupils have a well-rounded understanding of what they are learning.

As a maths leader, you might want to spend some time considering how fluency practice is taught in your school. What are the expectations for teachers? What changes would you want to see in the pupils' learning? There should be a balance between the underpinning conceptual understanding and the fact recall or procedure that sit above it. If you are using an 'off-the-shelf' curriculum product for maths, you may need to work with your colleagues to supplement it with additional fluency practice. Look for regular and structured practice where foundational concepts are repeated over time and there are daily or weekly opportunities to retrieve core concepts. Check how number bonds and times tables are taught within the scheme of work, and if there is a 'little and often' approach to secure them over time or if they are one-off lessons.

Developing fluency across the years

Fluency in EYFS

The Early Years are a vital time for pupils to develop number sense and fluency. There are key, foundational concepts that start here. Securing the principles of counting is integral in securing firm footing before building on these in KS1 and KS2.

Table 1 Comparing conceptual and procedural knowledge

<table>
<tr><th>PHASE</th><th>CONTEXT</th><th>CONCEPTUAL UNDERSTANDING</th><th>PROCEDURAL KNOWLEDGE</th></tr>
<tr><td rowspan="3">Key Stage 1 (KS1)</td><td rowspan="3">Subtracting two-digit numbers

For example:
42 – 19</td><td>Continual difference

Understanding that subtracting 20 is mentally easier than 19, so we can adjust the minuend (the number you subtract from) and subtrahend (the number you subtract) by the same amount to keep the difference the same:

$$\underset{-1}{42} - \underset{+1}{19}$$
$$41 - 20 = 21$$</td><td>Using a written method to calculate 42 – 19:

$$\begin{array}{r} {}^{3}\not{4}\;12 \\ -\;1\;\;9 \\ \hline 2\;\;3 \\ \hline \end{array}$$</td></tr>
<tr><td>Only using this strategy could lead to a lack of speed and accuracy when using larger numbers later.</td><td>Relying on this method, especially in KS1, could lead to errors in calculation or a lack of mental fluency.</td></tr>
<tr><td colspan="2">Your school's calculation policy should clarify whether or not column subtraction is a method used in KS1. To strike the balance between conceptual understanding and procedural knowledge when subtracting two-digit numbers, you could spend time exploring the concept of continual difference with concrete manipulative, e.g. Dienes blocks or on a number line. You will also probably spend time exploring other mental strategies. When the children are confidently using mental arithmetic strategies, you could then introduce the written method to increase efficiency, checking that the conceptual understanding is still there as you go.</td></tr>
</table>

<table>
<tr><th>PHASE</th><th>CONTEXT</th><th>CONCEPTUAL UNDERSTANDING</th><th>PROCEDURAL KNOWLEDGE</th></tr>
<tr><td rowspan="3">Key Stage 2 (KS2)</td><td rowspan="3">Dividing three-digit numbers by one-digit numbers

For example:

There are 145 pupils in Year 3. They are split equally into five classes.

How many pupils are in each class?</td><td>Quotitive division (sharing)

Understanding that 145 is being shared into five equal parts:
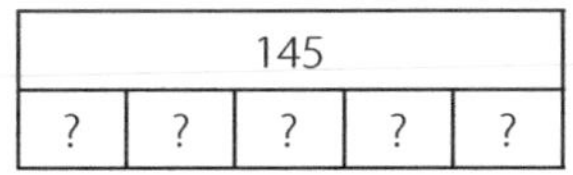

145 ÷ 5 = ?</td><td>Using a written method to calculate 145 ÷ 5:

$\begin{array}{r|rrr} & 0 & 2 & 9 \\ \hline 5 & 1 & {}^{1}4 & {}^{4}5 \end{array}$</td></tr>
<tr><td>While bar models support the conceptual structure of sharing, they don't support calculating the quotient.</td><td>Relying on this method in isolation could lead to a lack of understanding about what the parts of the calculation mean.</td></tr>
<tr><td colspan="2">Like the KS1 example, your school's calculation policy should give teachers an insight into when short division is taught. To strike the balance between the conceptual understanding of quotitive division and the use of short division to calculate, you could teach the structures of partitive and quotitive division and then give the pupils multiple example word problems to sketch out in a bar model. This will check their understanding of the problems and the two structures of division. Then, when they know the difference and can unpack what a problem is asking, you can teach the written method to improve efficient calculation.</td></tr>
</table>

The principles of counting (Gelman and Gallistel, 1978) are:

- cardinality: using the last number when counting to indicate the total number of items in a group
- one-to-one correspondence: assigning one number name per item in a group
- stable order: keeping a stable and correct verbal counting sequence
- order irrelevance: understanding that the order which items are counted in is not significant and the total number doesn't change
- abstraction: knowing that it isn't just physical things that can be counted.

Along with this, being able to subitise is equally important. 'Subitising' comes from the Latin word *subitus*, which means 'sudden'. Subitising is being able to recognise and name how many items are in a group immediately, without counting (Clements, 1999). Young children must develop this kind of number sense as a foundation for more complex number work later.

Perceptual subitising

Perceptual subitising is being able to identify and name quickly how many are in a group up to five without counting. Any more than five requires us to chunk

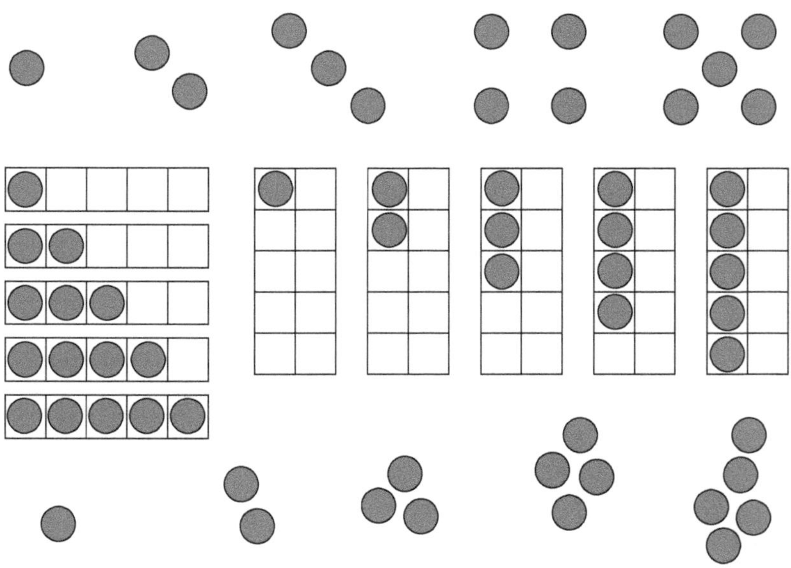

Figure 5.1 Counters in groups of up to five, arranged using dice patterns, five frames, ten frames and random arrangements

the group up. You might show pupils numbers up to five using dice patterns, counters within five frames or ten frames, or in random arrangements.

Conceptual subitising

Conceptual subitising is when we break a group into smaller groups, identify the quantity in each group and then combine them without counting individual items.

For example, you might see this representation of seven and chunk the counters into groups of five and two.

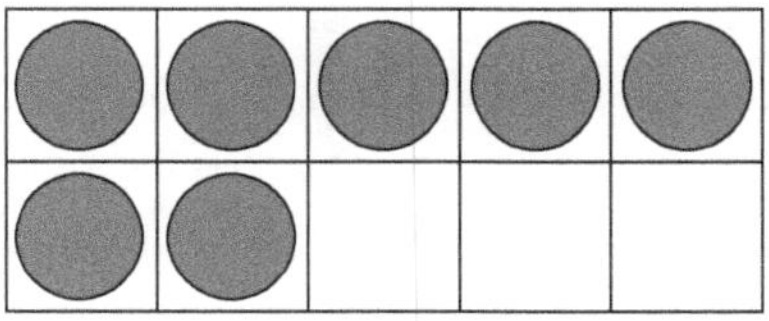

Figure 5.2 Seven counters in a ten-frame, in two rows of five and two

Or, you might see this representation of seven and chunk the counters into groups of three and four.

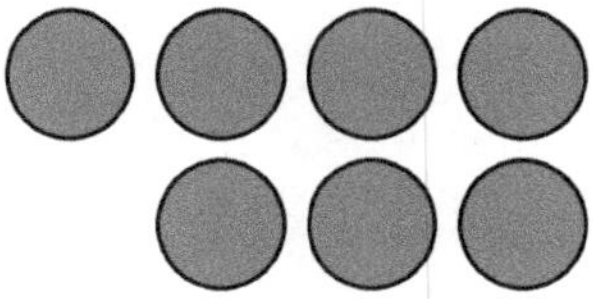

Figure 5.3 Seven counters, in two rows of four and three

As a maths subject leader, make sure that you work alongside your EYFS team to ensure that the pupils are getting opportunities to count numbers to 20, explore numbers to 10 in more depth, and develop their number sense through subitising. Off the shelf schemes of work should be compliant with the early learning goals, but as the subject leader you may want to quality assure this alongside staff in EYFS. Not everyone is an EYFS expert (me included!), so look for a focus on exploring cardinality and counting, composition of numbers including part-whole relationships, rich use of concrete manipulatives and high-quality pictorial representations, exploring pattern and ample opportunity to subitise. If you aren't sure how the youngest learners in your school develop their number sense, then make sure you get into EYFS and see it in action. Some of the best practice happens in EYFS and you don't want to miss it!

Early maths researcher, Clements (1999), concludes that pupils can develop their unitising and counting skills, and their understanding of the composition of number through pattern recognition and subitising. Spending time on subitising positively impacts their fluency and number sense.

Consider how you want subitising to be taught and practised in your school. Will your EYFS pupils do five minutes of subitising a day? Short, daily practice is more effective than longer less frequent sessions. Subitising activities can be woven into daily routines such as a whole-class carpet activity after break or lunch times or after the register. What tasks would you want those EYFS pupils to participate in? You might use flash cards (both physical and digital) using structured visual patterns that encourage number recognition, tasks that encourage discussion by asking 'How do you know?' and tasks that involve comparing the same quantity with different representations such as dots, fingers and cubes. You know your context best, but if you want to get to know it even better, you could drop into EYFS to observe how confidently children can recognise small quantities without counting and use formative assessment like 'Show me five' to gauge the impact of what is currently happening. Below are some ideas for subitising.

- Throw up to five pebbles into a tray and have the pupils subitise the quantity.
- Briefly flash an image on the screen and have pupils shout out the quantity.
- As above, but this time ask pupils to show you on their fingers (even better if their hands are above their heads).
- Show counters in a five or ten frame and have the pupils say the number out loud.
- Ask pupils to match visual representations of numbers with the numerals.
- Play dice games, for example snakes and ladders, and have the pupils subitise each number rather than count it.
- Play 'subitising bingo': the pupils have bingo grids with numerals, you flash up a representation and they mark the number on their grids.

Fluency in Key Stage 1

Fluency in KS1 lays the foundation for mathematical competence, enabling pupils to tackle calculations confidently, reason logically and solve problems as they progress. Key fluency elements in KS1 include (DfE, 2013):

- recall and use of number bonds (within 10 and then 20)
- addition and subtraction facts to 20, including related facts up to 100
- understanding of place value (tens and ones)
- fluent use of mental calculation strategies (e.g. bridging through 10, doubles/near doubles)
- introduction to multiplication and division facts (especially 2, 5 and 10 times tables)
- flexible thinking – being able to adapt known facts (e.g. knowing 3 + 4 helps with 30 + 40)
- fluent reading and writing of numbers, including comparing and ordering
- reasonable efficiency – choosing and using strategies that are appropriate to the calculation context.

Developing fluency at this stage focuses on fostering a deep understanding of number, embedding essential skills through engaging, well-structured practice. Rosenshine (2012) emphasises the importance of frequent, varied practice and scaffolding, where new learning builds on prior knowledge. Regular retrieval practice also helps secure facts in long-term memory, preventing forgetting and fostering automaticity.

Pupils in KS1 build fluency by experiencing and exploring a range of representations with concrete manipulatives, as well as pictorially and in abstract forms too. For example, pupils may use counters on ten frames to explore addition, transition to drawing representations, and translate this into written number sentences.

As a maths leader, collaborate with your KS1 teams on how to embed fluency practice. A 'little and often' approach with ten minutes of number bonds and counting per day might be enough to secure these concepts in your KS1 pupils. Or you might want to do one longer fluency session per week with shorter bursts of fluency practice on the other days to embed what was covered in the longer session. This decision may be influenced by the capacity within the weekly timetable. Some schools have greater flexibility than others, so you need to do what works for you and the KS1 teachers! Fluency sessions in KS1 might include:

- subitising – you can use the activities from the EYFS section on subitising, working within a ten frame and using conceptual subitising to group larger quantities of dots or cubes

- singing – you could use the BBC Supermovers songs or 'Ten Sleepy Fingers'
- flashcards – for example, you could have seven on one side and three on the other and the pupils have to shout the corresponding number based on the bond you are working on
- 'Fluent in 5' – you could put five arithmetic questions up on the board each morning for early work, working on the same style of questions for five days in a row with the numbers changing each day. Third Space Learning have a 'Fluent in 5' programme, *Vocabulary Ninja* has 'Fluent Five' and many schools make their own based on what their pupils need.

Fluency in Lower Key Stage 2

Fluency in Lower Key Stage 2 (LKS2) expands beyond number bonds, to applying them and using efficient strategies for calculating, deepening understanding of place value and developing flexibility in problem solving contexts. Times tables are hugely important in LKS2, as is the ability to use them to derive related facts.

One of the drawbacks of many off-the-shelf schemes of work is the lack of provision for times table practice and embedding times tables knowledge over time. There might be lesson materials for teaching the times table, but a one-off lesson on each times table is not enough to secure times tables in our pupils. Sometimes the schemes only provide one lesson to the 3s, one to the 4s and one to the 8s in Year 3. This leads to teachers having an 'I've taught the times tables' mentality, so you may want to consider what your school's supplementary teaching and practice programme looks like for times tables so that the pupils can recall them quickly and accurately. It is worth mentioning that in England, pupils at the end of Year 4 sit the Multiplication Tables Check (MTC) which gives the pupils six seconds per question, so the pupils should be used to answering questions in this timeframe. Programmes like 'Times Table Rockstars' are great for practising the tables once they have been taught. Fluency sessions in LKS2 might include:

- activities from KS1
- chanting multiples of 3, 4, 6, 7, 8, 9, 25, 50, 100 and 1,000
- using a counting stick and sticky notes to practise times tables
- call and repeat choral work or times table ping pong

- speed recall of times tables and bonds within 100
- mini quizzes to practise key arithmetic methods
- 'ten in 10' (ten arithmetic questions).

Fluency in Upper Key Stage 2

In Upper Key Stage 2 (UKS2), fluency is about increasing efficiency and sophistication. Pupils extend their understanding to larger numbers, more complex operations and make connections across mathematical areas, such as fractions, decimals, percentages and ratio. Pupils will develop a deeper understanding of a variety of areas within maths and therefore need to be fluent with number to open up space in the working memory to solve problems, make connections and reason about their learning.

In UKS2, you can see the impact of effective fluency teaching when the pupils are encountering algebra, ratio and proportion, and converting fractions into decimals and percentages. Laying the foundation for fluency until this point can help to lower pupils' cognitive load when learning new concepts. Where they are already working fluently with numbers, pupils are more able to apply this to new learning and be able to take on new procedures or skills without being weighed down by needing to think hard to recall facts. Fluency sessions in UKS2 might include:

- activities from KS1 and LKS2
- times table and other key facts recall
- balancing equations, e.g. $42 \times 4 = \_\_\_ \times 8$
- multiplying and dividing by powers of ten
- mental arithmetic strategies, e.g. compensation.

Daily practice and spaced retrieval

Daily practice sessions might focus on fact recall or practice of certain operations. In contrast, spaced retrieval requires revisiting concepts over time leaving increasing intervals as times goes on. Daily practice helps to embed essential skills into long-term memory, while spaced retrieval strengthens these connections over time. Regular opportunities to revisit key concepts ensure pupils retain knowledge and can apply it flexibly.

You might encourage your teachers to have a dedicated daily fluency activity, such as quick-fire number bonds, times table recall or mental arithmetic. You might also want to look at the curriculum and consider how you could incorporate questions that revisit previous topics to reinforce earlier learning alongside new content. It will also be important to develop the use of informal, low-stakes quizzes to highlight key concepts and encourage pupils to monitor their progress over time.

Example PD session: teaching fluency

Here is an example of what a PD session on fluency teaching could look like.

TIMING SUGGESTION	SESSION GUIDANCE
10 mins	• Use the misconceptions about fluency from earlier in the chapter as the basis for a 'True or False?' quiz for teachers at the start of the session. • Encourage them to answer first and then discuss/debate in small groups.

15 mins	• Think-Pair-Share: Ask teachers to reflect on their own experiences of fluency in maths. Did they focus on speed and recall, or was there an emphasis on understanding? How do their current fluency practices in the classroom align with their own experiences?
	• Introduce the three key components of fluency:
	  • Accuracy: performing calculations correctly.
	  • Efficiency: choosing appropriate strategies and using minimal steps.
	  • Flexibility: applying number knowledge in different contexts.
	• Discuss common misconceptions about fluency, including:
	  • 'Fluency = speed.'
	  • 'Fluency applies only to arithmetic.'
	  • 'Only high-attaining pupils can be fluent.'

15 mins	• In phase teams, teachers reflect on the fluency strategies they currently use. What fluency routines do they have in place? Are these strategies supporting conceptual understanding or just recall?
	• Ask each group to write examples of fluency activities on sticky notes and categorise them:
	  • Promotes fluency with deep understanding.
	  • Relies on memorisation alone.
	  • Needs adapting to be more effective.

TIMING SUGGESTION	SESSION GUIDANCE

15 mins	• Present examples of effective fluency sessions:
	  • EYFS – subitising games, counting principles, one more/one less activities.
	  • KS1 – number bonds practice, part-whole models, fluency through stories.
	  • LKS2 – counting sticks, times table challenges, ten-minute fluency tasks.
	  • UKS2 – mental arithmetic challenges, rapid recall of derived facts.
	• Ask teachers to work in pairs to plan a ten minute daily fluency session that is appropriate for their class.

15 mins	• Prompt teachers to discuss how fluency should progress across year groups and identify gaps.
	• Create a fluency progression map:
	  • What are the non-negotiable fluency expectations in each phase?
	  • How can fluency be embedded within lessons, not just in separate sessions?
	  • What does each year group need to achieve by the end of it?
	• Agree on one fluency focus to develop over the next term, e.g. increasing retrieval opportunities.

After the session	• Create a shared fluency document outlining key expectations across phases. • Offer coaching or team planning sessions to refine fluency strategies. • Monitor fluency implementation through lesson drop-ins and book looks. • Provide teachers with additional fluency resources for structured variation and retrieval practice.

Case study: introducing subitising

Nisha is the maths subject leader at a three-form-entry school in a large city. She has been the maths leader for two years and has spent most of her time focusing on KS2 maths. When reviewing Early Years fluency provision, she notices that although counting is well established and children appear to have a stable order and understand cardinality, they don't appear to know one more or one less and can't recognise small numbers instantly.

Nisha books herself onto a free EYFS work group with the local maths hub to improve her knowledge. There, she learns that subitising is an important part of early number fluency. She chooses to tackle subitising in her school so that children leave EYFS with better number sense and ready for Year 1 maths.

To begin, Nisha drops into all Reception classes during morning maths. She does this across a two-week period so that she gets a range of snapshots instead of seeing a one-off session. Nisha notices that while teachers regularly use ten frames to count, they rarely ask children to instantly recognise quantities without counting. Nisha carries out informal 'Show me five' formative assessments to gauge confidence in perceptual subitising. Out of 28 children, seven of them were confidently and quickly able to recognise numbers one to five, 12 of them could do it after a longer period of time, and nine of them were not able to recognise the numbers.

Nisha approaches her SLT and asks for time to deliver a PD session for EYFS staff. SLT suggest that all teachers come along, not just EYFS, so that everyone can get a better understanding of the foundations of early maths. They book this in for next term. Nisha goes through:

- what subitising is
- the difference between perceptual and conceptual subitising
- why subitising should be taught daily in short bursts
- examples of effective activities such as flashing dot patterns, using fingers above heads.

As a team, the staff come up with a plan of action to work on subitising. Nisha creates a bank of subitising flashcards and simple ten-frame images, and arranges a time to model a subitising session using these resources in each Reception class. Each Reception teacher agrees to introduce five minutes of subitising practice daily straight after morning registration. They agree to use consistent language: 'How do you know?' and 'Can you see it another way?'.

At the start of the next week, Nisha models the subitising sessions in all three classes with some teachers and teaching assistants from KS1 and KS2 coming to watch too. Over the next three weeks, she drops into each Reception class multiple times to evaluate the impact of the subitising sessions.

After half a term, Nisha reassesses children using the same 'Show me...' prompts. The proportion of children confidently recognising quantities to five without counting increases from seven out of 28 to 15 out of 28. Teachers report that children are more secure with composition of number and more confident in counting on. Nisha plans to build on this success by introducing more conceptual subitising activities in the next term.

By focusing on subitising, Nisha ensures all children in EYFS develop a secure number sense foundation, supporting fluency in later key stages. Staff feel more confident about daily fluency routines and understand why subitising matters.

Questions for reflection

- Does fluency in our school strike the right balance between conceptual understanding and procedural knowledge?
- What strategies could we implement to provide daily practice and spaced retrieval opportunities for pupils across all year groups?
- How do we monitor and support teachers to embed fluency teaching into their lessons? What PD might they need?

Explore further

- Third Space Learning's blog *What Is Fluency In Maths & How Do Schools Develop It?* (2025) by Rebecca Jakes: https://thirdspacelearning.com/blog/what-is-fluency-in-maths-definition-ks2/
- NRICH's article *Developing Number Fluency – What, Why and How* (2014) by Lynne McClure: https://nrich.maths.org/articles/developing-number-fluency-what-why-and-how

Chapter summary

- Fluency in maths is the ability to work with numbers accurately, efficiently and flexibly.
- Misconceptions surrounding fluency include fluency equalling speed, rote learning and mastery, that only high prior attainers can be fluent or that low prior attainers can only do fluency work, that fluency is just arithmetic or that it comes easily.
- Fluency requires conceptual understanding and procedural knowledge.
- EYFS lays the foundation for fluency through subitising, the five principles of counting and developing number sense.
- In KS1, pupils develop fluency with number bonds and mental arithmetic strategies.
- In KS2, pupils develop fluency with times tables and written arithmetic strategies.
- You may want teachers to have daily fluency practice to supplement the scheme of work in place at your school.

6 Reasoning

Reasoning is the key to unlocking mathematical understanding. It requires a deep understanding of the subject matter so that pupils can make generalisations and conjectures, find patterns and connections between concepts, explain methods and processes, and justify conclusions logically. This chapter will look at misconceptions about reasoning and reasoning in EYFS, KS1 and KS2. It will look at supporting pupils with special educational needs and disabilities (SEND) and pupils for whom English is an additional language (EAL). It will also look at how to lead reasoning across the school.

Misconceptions about reasoning

- **'Reasoning is only for higher-attaining pupils.'** This stems from reasoning tasks being used as extensions or 'challenge questions' rather than as a core part of every child's mathematical journey. All pupils should be supported to reason to deepen their learning.
- **'Reasoning happens after fluency.'** While fluency and reasoning are, of course, linked, you do not need to wait until a child is fluent in a concept before asking questions that prompt mathematical thinking. Spotting patterns, making predictions or justifying methods all help to embed pupils' understanding and strengthen fluency.
- **'Reasoning means writing an explanation.'** While written explanations can show reasoning, it's not the only way. Pupils can reason through diagrams, manipulatives, classroom talk or choosing efficient methods. Overemphasis on writing can limit opportunities and disadvantage some learners.
- **'Reasoning is just about word problems.'** Although reasoning is important in problem solving, it's broader than that. It includes generalising, identifying patterns, justifying ideas, disproving statements and comparing methods, not just tackling worded questions.
- **'You have to know the answer before you can reason.'** Reasoning is not just about explaining a correct answer. It also includes exploring possibilities, testing ideas or spotting when something doesn't work. It's a tool for thinking through maths, not just reporting on it.

- **'You can't assess reasoning.'** While it is less straightforward than marking a string of arithmetic questions, reasoning can be assessed through observation, classroom talk or journal jottings.
- **'Maths is about getting the answer right.'** It would be silly to suggest that we don't want pupils to answer questions correctly, but placing an emphasis on the answer rather than the thinking and the journey can restrict how willing pupils are to explore and try things out.

Developing reasoning across the years

A common misconception about reasoning is that only 'more able' or 'greater depth' pupils can move onto reasoning. The truth is that all pupils can and should be given the opportunity to engage in reasoning and mathematical thinking in every single lesson, regardless of prior attainment. Nunes et al. (2009) highlighted mathematical reasoning as the most significant factor influencing a pupil's success in maths, so it is essential that we embed opportunities for developing reasoning skills throughout the curriculum for all pupils.

Reasoning in EYFS

Some of the best practice happens in our EYFS classrooms. Pupils in EYFS spend lots of time exploring and talking about what they are doing. They are most likely engaging in mathematical reasoning more than any other phase in the school. Staff in EYFS ask questions such as 'Why did that happen?' or 'How do you know?' throughout the day, either during a maths-focused teaching input or during continuous provision where pupils are exploring number and numerical structure through practical and real-world activities.

In your role as the maths subject leader, work with your EYFS colleagues to ensure that their classrooms are full of mathematically-rich talk right from the start so that KS1 teachers can build on this. If you haven't yet been able to spend time in EYFS either as a teacher yourself or as the maths lead, spend time in EYFS so that you can see how maths learning is planned and structured. After observing your EYFS colleagues in action, why not swap classes with them for a lesson or part of the day so that you have first-hand experience of finding those opportunities for reasoning? While it *could* feel disruptive to your own class having someone else teaching them, sometimes we have to look at the long-term and wider impact that actions like this will have. It also gives your EYFS colleague a chance to experience maths in another part of the school. Consider setting up peer observations, a valuable PD activity for your KS1 and KS2 teachers, so that everyone sees how reasoning is done in EYFS. Some schools have an open-door policy where they can go in and out of each other's lessons for professional development, as long as their own class is covered and working well. This isn't practical for everyone! You could ask your EYFS staff to give a selection of dates and times that would work for them and have people sign up to see EYFS in action. Generally, pupils in EYFS are so independent and focused on what they're doing that they don't mind extra adults coming in.

In effective EYFS classrooms, reasoning and mathematical thinking is happening constantly. Staff ask questions to pull out the mathematical thinking and they encourage their pupils to be curious by finding patterns, solving problems and more. Here are some examples of what sort of reasoning might happen in an EYFS classroom.

In practice: mathematical reasoning in EYFS

TASK	MODEL	QUESTIONS
Spotting a repeating pattern	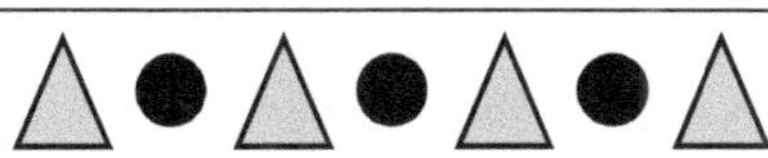 **Figure 6.1** Row of six alternating triangles and circles	• What comes next? • How do you know?
Making ten with two colour counters on a ten frame	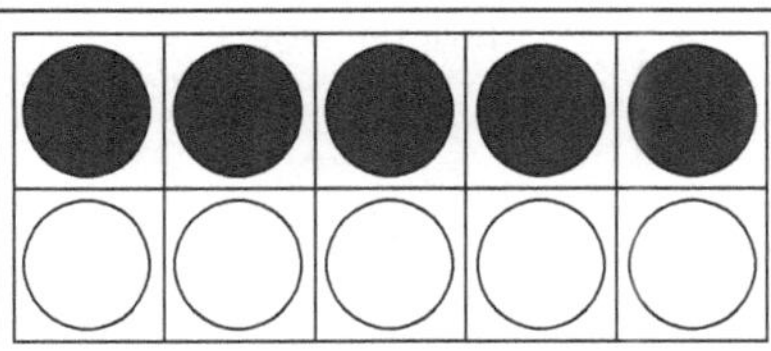 **Figure 6.2** Five black and five white counters in a ten frame	• How do you know that makes ten? • Is there another way to do it? • How do you know you have found all of the solutions?
Sorting buttons	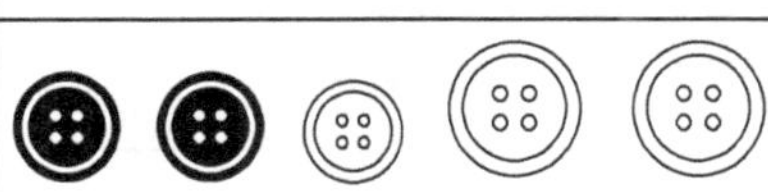 **Figure 6.3** Five buttons: two small black, one small white and two large white	• How will you sort them? • How are they different? • Why is this button in this group? • Why is this button not in this group?

Making shapes with pipe cleaners	 **Figure 6.4** Roughly drawn triangle, square and circle	• Which shapes can you make? • How do you know you've made a triangle?

Reasoning in Key Stage 1 and Key Stage 2

In KS1, teachers can build on the verbal reasoning done in EYFS. They can also start to consider how to phase in written reasoning. KS1 is where we can teach good habits for jotting and writing down conjectures, which is important for writing explanations and justifications later in KS2.

Reasoning shouldn't be specific tasks plonked at the end of independent practice because not all pupils will necessarily finish their independent work, and therefore might never experience reasoning. Some low prior attainers may never get to the reasoning tasks, which could leave them with huge gaps in understanding. Mathematical reasoning should run through every part of a maths lesson so that all pupils can think deeply about what they are learning throughout the sequence. As stated by Willingham (2009, p.47) 'memory is the residue of thought.' We remember the things we think hard about, therefore pupils are more likely to learn and remember what they have thought about, so these opportunities must be presented to all pupils throughout a lesson. Empower your teachers to plan lessons that encourage the pupils to ask questions, notice patterns and make generalisations.

In practice: reasoning in KS1 and KS2

Here are some examples of how you can weave reasoning into lessons in KS1 and KS2.

TASK	QUESTION TYPE	PROMPT
Practising number bonds to nine	Odd one out	2+7 3+6 1+8 9+1 Which sum is the odd one out? Why?
Learning about the properties of 2D shapes	True or false	True or false: All 2D shapes have straight sides.

<table>
<tr><td>Comparing two representations of the same data</td><td>What is the same and what is different?</td><td>
<table>
<tr><th>Jam flavour</th><th>Number of children</th></tr>
<tr><td>Strawberry</td><td>4</td></tr>
<tr><td>Raspberry</td><td>8</td></tr>
<tr><td>Plum</td><td>5</td></tr>
</table>
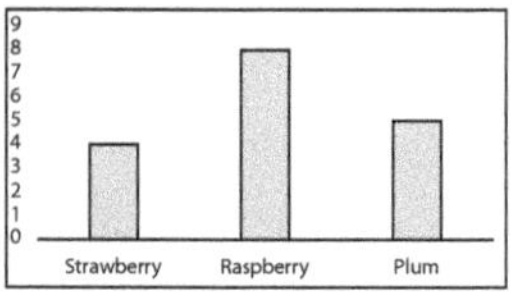

Figure 6.5 Table and bar chart showing jam flavour preferences</td></tr>
<tr><td>Using related facts to solve calculations</td><td>What do you notice?</td><td>$36 \times 10 = 360$
$3.6 \times 10 = 36$</td></tr>
<tr><td>Learning about efficient division methods</td><td>Rank by difficulty</td><td>896÷8 9,609÷3 30÷5
1,257÷6 374÷9</td></tr>
<tr><td>Learning about the relationship between the number of sides and the sum of interior angles of polygons</td><td>What happens if...?</td><td>

Figure 6.6 Triangle, square, pentagon and hexagon marked with sums of interior angles; heptagon marked with question mark</td></tr>
</table>

This is just a tiny set of examples that can be used at the point of teaching new concepts to spark conversation and conjecturing, or later during application of new concepts. The pupils will, of course, need some explicit instruction around the new concept as well, but it doesn't always have to be before they have had a chance to think and notice for themselves. As the maths leader of your school, you might want to look at when your pupils get the chance to think and talk mathematically, and work with your colleagues on developing lesson structures that allow for this flexibility.

Strategies to develop reasoning

It is important for maths leaders to develop a culture of mathematical reasoning in their schools. A lot of this is down to the teachers' own relationships with maths and how they model this to their pupils, but it starts with you as the subject leader and will hopefully filter down to the teachers too.

Modelling mathematical talk

Mathematical talk is a powerful tool for developing reasoning. When pupils are encouraged to articulate their thinking when working on questions that require reasoning, they can deepen their understanding. Creating a classroom culture that prioritises mathematical talk ensures that pupils see maths as an exploratory subject rather than one where the focus is solely on getting the right answer.

It can sometimes be difficult to take yourself out of the expert shoes that you walk in as a teacher and deliberately put yourself in the shoes of novices, but for teachers to create a culture of curiosity about maths effectively, they need to model thinking aloud and keep asking 'why?'. For the pupils in your school to feel confident to share ideas and thoughts, justify their thinking and challenge others, they need to have seen it in action.

Teachers can model the messy thinking by showing and telling the pupils what they can see. This can be difficult for someone who is at the point of automaticity and perhaps hasn't had to break things down like this before. As maths lead, invite your colleagues into your lessons, go in and teach their classes or deliver PD on this, to show them how you can explicitly model this kind of curiosity and active noticing. Some colleagues might benefit from one-to-one or small group coaching on how to do this.

Model using sentence stems like, 'I notice that...', 'This reminds me of...' or 'I wonder if...' to demonstrate what thinking mathematically can look like.

In practice: reasoning sentence stems

Here is a simple progression of reasoning sentence stems that you could introduce in your school:

PHASE	SENTENCE STEMS
EYFS	I know... because... I think... because...
KS1	I know... so... First, I... then I...
KS2	If I know... then I know... I noticed that... This works because... We can prove it by...

And here is an example of how to use them in a lesson:

PHASE	CONTEXT	SENTENCE STEM	SCRIPT
EYFS	**Comparing quantities using subitising** The teacher is using dot patterns to help pupils compare between two quantities without counting.	'I know… because…'	Teacher shows two cards – one with 4 dots and one with 2 dots. 'Look at both cards. Which one has more?' Teacher gives time for pupils to process the question. 'Let's use our reasoning sentence. I know… because…' 'For example, I know that the first card has more because I can see 4 dots and only 2 dots on the other card.'
KS1	**Bridging to ten** The class is exploring different ways to make 14 using two parts. The teacher is modelling the method aloud.	'I know… so…'	Teacher writes 6 + ? = 14 on the board. 'We're working out what goes with 6 to make 14.' 'Let's use our reasoning sentence. I know… so…' 'For example, I know that 6 and 4 make 10, so I need 4 more to get to 14. I have added two lots of 4 so the missing number is 8.'
KS2	**Comparing fractions with different denominators** The class is comparing $\frac{3}{4}$ with $\frac{5}{8}$. The teacher is modelling how to reason using equivalent fractions.	'I noticed that…'	The teacher writes $\frac{3}{4}$ and $\frac{5}{8}$ on the board. 'Which is greater?' 'Let's use our reasoning sentence. I noticed that…' 'For example, I noticed that $\frac{3}{4}$ is equivalent to $\frac{6}{8}$, so I know that it is greater than $\frac{5}{8}$.'

By using these stems, pupils learn to organise their thoughts, share their reasoning, and build on others' ideas. Over time, this practice also supports their development of precise mathematical vocabulary and deeper conceptual understanding which will enable them to reason more deeply.

Mathematically-rich and open-ended tasks

Mathematically-rich and open-ended tasks are tasks that encourage exploration, flexibility and deeper understanding by allowing pupils to approach problems in different ways. Tasks like these encourage mathematical dialogue, where pupils can explain their strategies, learn from others and refine their thinking. Mathematically-rich tasks also naturally differentiate learning, as they provide multiple entry points and opportunities for extension. These low-threshold, high-ceiling tasks mean that all pupils can access the learning while some pupils might explore deeper structures and generalisations. This inclusivity ensures that all pupils benefit from the challenge and depth that rich tasks offer.

In practice: example mathematically-rich and open-ended tasks

Here are some examples of mathematically-rich or open-ended tasks:

PHASE	CONTEXT	TASK
EYFS	**Exploring properties of shapes** Pupils can choose their own sorting criteria and adults can guide or prompt by asking questions like 'Why did you put these shapes together?'. Low-threshold: pupils can begin by matching or naming shapes. High-ceiling: pupils can use language like 'sides' or 'corners' and may sort in a variety of ways.	'Sort these shapes.' Provide children with a variety of 2D shapes, including circles, triangles and rectangles, in different sizes and colours.

KS1	**Doubling within 20** Pupils can use physical resources to explore doubling in a concrete way and are encouraged to reason about doubling. Low-threshold: pupils can match and identify doubles using domino tiles. High-ceiling: some pupils may spot patterns such as all doubles are even, or begin to use known facts to predict or generalise.	'I've found a domino where both ends are the same. What numbers can you double with dominoes? Can you find them all?' Give children domino tiles or printed versions.
KS2	**Properties of number** This promotes reasoning and justification from multiple perspectives and allows for deeper exploration. Low-threshold: pupils can identify simple differences, e.g. 45 is the only odd number. High-ceiling: pupils may look for common factors and see that while nine goes into them all, only 45 is a multiple of five.	'Which of these numbers is the odd one out: 18, 36, 45, 72? And why?' There is no single correct answer. The children can explain their thinking.

The importance of mistakes

Mistakes are an inevitable part of learning maths, and when handled effectively, they can play a role in deepening understanding. Instead of being seen as setbacks, mistakes can be framed as opportunities for growth and exploration. By creating a classroom culture where errors are valued, pupils are encouraged to take risks, learn from their misconceptions and develop stronger reasoning skills. A valuable technique for using mistakes is error analysis, where teachers model reasoning through incorrect solutions. For example, after solving a problem incorrectly on purpose, the teacher might ask pupils to identify why it's incorrect and where it went wrong.

In practice: looking at mistakes with pupils

Problem: Amir is saving up for a new bike. He earns £12 per week from his paper round. He already has £48 saved. The bike costs £132. How many more weeks does he need to work to buy the bike?

The teacher models while narrating what they are doing.

'Let's break this down. Amir earns £12 per week and he needs £132. First, I'll add £48 and £132. That gives me £180. Next, I'll divide £180 by £12 to find out how many weeks he needs to work: 180 divided by 12 is 15, so Amir needs to work for 15 weeks. Done!'

The teacher pauses and looks uncertain.

'Have I gone wrong somewhere?'

The teacher invites responses from pupils, paraphrasing and guiding them to focus on the structure of the problem.

'Work out the answer to this problem in pairs. Use these stem sentences while you talk it out: I know that… I notice that… First, I need to… then…'

The teacher circulates the classroom, listening to the pupils using the sentence stems. Then, they ask different pairs to contribute what they said.

The teacher asks some follow-up questions:

'Why do you think I made that mistake?'

'What part of the question helped us to realise something wasn't quite right?'

'How can we check our answer makes sense in the context?'

By modelling unpacking the error with the class, pupils can learn to spot common pitfalls, evaluate the logic of their methods and refine their strategies.

Mistakes also provide opportunities to highlight and address misconceptions. If several pupils in the class make similar errors, this can signal an area that requires revisiting or further clarification. Turning these patterns of errors into teachable moments helps pupils see that misunderstandings are normal and part of the learning process. For this approach to be successful, it is essential to foster a safe and supportive classroom environment. Pupils need to feel comfortable sharing their work and confident that their mistakes will be met with encouragement rather than criticism. Teachers can reinforce this by celebrating effort, emphasising progress and modelling a positive attitude toward challenges.

One strategy you could implement in your school is a routine for responding to other pupils' answers. This ensures that everyone is listening and participating, but it also encourages everyone to look out actively for mistakes that can then be used as teaching points. Here is an example of such a routine:

- If the pupils agree with the answer, the pupils pat their shoulders.
- If the pupils don't agree or want to challenge the answer, they put their finger on their nose.
- If they want to build on the given answer, they motion building blocks with their hands.

Supporting pupils with SEND

Mathematical reasoning can be a challenge for all pupils and it may be particularly demanding for some pupils with SEND. However, with the right strategies and adaptations, all pupils can participate successfully and make progress in reasoning. Reasoning helps pupils deepen their conceptual understanding and develop transferable problem-solving skills, so ensuring inclusivity in reasoning tasks is essential.

It is important to acknowledge that every pupil is different, and every additional need is unique. There is no single approach that will work for all pupils. Equally, having a diagnosis or being on the SEND register does not automatically mean a pupil requires differentiated learning in every maths lesson.

An inclusive approach to reasoning starts with designing lessons that remove unnecessary barriers for all pupils. Many of the adaptations that make reasoning more accessible for pupils with SEND, such as the use of visuals, structured stem sentences, concrete manipulatives and clear routines, are equally beneficial for the other pupils and harmful to none. This principle of inclusivity by design ensures that effective support is embedded into everyday practice rather than added as an afterthought. For example, just as a visual timetable benefits the whole class, clear visual models and structured prompts for reasoning support every learner to access and articulate mathematical thinking.

Visual aids, concrete manipulatives and scaffolding

Using visual aids and concrete manipulatives is one way of activating learning for all pupils, especially some pupils with SEND. Tools such as bar models, number lines and Dienes allow pupils to see the structure of a problem rather than relying solely on abstract reasoning. For example, when solving a division problem, pupils could use counters to group items physically, helping them understand the concept of sharing or grouping.

Scaffolding is also crucial for pupils with SEND. Teachers can provide step-by-step instructions, worked examples, or backwards-faded tasks where they start with a fully complete example, and gradually the steps of the method are removed one question at a time to guide pupils through the process. Gradually removing scaffolds as pupils gain confidence fosters independence while ensuring they feel supported at each stage.

Alternative communication methods

For pupils who struggle with verbal or written explanations, offering alternative ways to communicate their reasoning is essential. Drawing diagrams and using manipulatives can allow these pupils to demonstrate their thinking without the added pressure of language. For instance, a pupil might use counters to show how they grouped numbers in a multiplication problem or draw a visual representation to explain a concept.

Encouraging all pupils to use these alternative methods can build confidence, showing pupils that their reasoning is valued regardless of how it is expressed. Teachers can complement these approaches with verbal prompts or sentence starters to help pupils gradually build their communication skills.

Breaking tasks into smaller steps

Reasoning tasks can sometimes feel overwhelming for pupils with SEND, particularly if they involve multiple steps or abstract ideas. Breaking these tasks into smaller, manageable parts makes them more accessible. For example, rather than asking a pupil to solve a multi-step problem all at once, teachers can guide them through one part of the process before moving on to the next.

Supporting EAL pupils

Pupils who are learning English as an additional language bring unique strengths and challenges to reasoning tasks in maths. While their understanding of mathematical concepts may be strong, language barriers can hinder their ability to articulate reasoning or access problem-solving tasks fully, which will be covered in Chapter 7. By providing targeted support, teachers can help pupils learning EAL to engage in mathematical reasoning confidently.

Visual aids and collaborative tasks

Visual aids are invaluable for pupils learning EAL, as they reduce the reliance on language and allow pupils to access tasks through visual understanding. Diagrams and manipulatives provide representations that support reasoning. For example, a part-whole cherry model can help pupils understand part-whole relationships without needing extensive verbal explanations.

Collaborative tasks are another effective strategy. Working in pairs or small groups gives pupils learning EAL the chance to hear mathematical language used in context, observe reasoning processes and contribute their ideas without needing to rely solely on individual responses. When these pupils are paired up or working in a group, they can use concrete manipulatives or pictorial representations alongside their verbal and written reasoning.

Vocabulary banks and sentence stems

Mathematical reasoning relies heavily on language, making it crucial to provide pupils learning EAL with the tools they need to communicate effectively. Vocabulary banks, with visuals and key terms such as 'greater than', 'difference' or 'equal to', can help pupils learn and use precise mathematical language. Displaying these terms in the classroom when teaching them or having them on hand on word mats and revisiting them frequently ensures they are accessible and reinforced over time. As well as vocabulary, sentence stems provide a structured way for pupils learning EAL to articulate their reasoning. Phrases such as 'I think this because…' or 'This is similar to…' offer frameworks for expressing ideas, reducing the cognitive load associated with formulating complete responses. Over time, pupils learning EAL can adapt these stems to their own language, building confidence and fluency.

Case study: embedding stem sentences to enhance mathematical reasoning

As the maths subject leader at her school, Sindi-Kate identifies a significant challenge that many pupils struggle to articulate their mathematical thinking clearly. Despite showing strong understanding of mathematical concepts in fluency practice, they face difficulty in expressing their reasoning. This creates a barrier to full engagement in deeper mathematical discussions and, in turn, hinders their progression in both reasoning and problem-solving skills.

To address this, Sindi-Kate focuses on embedding the use of stem sentences across the school. These sentences provide a foundation that pupils can modify and expand upon as they develop their reasoning skills, making it easier for them to share their ideas and justify their answers. Before implementing this strategy with the pupils, Sindi-Kate holds a PD session with the teaching staff. During the session, she introduces the concept of mathematical talk and its role in developing reasoning. She discusses how sentence stems can provide the scaffolding necessary for pupils, especially those with lower levels of language proficiency, to communicate their ideas effectively.

She finds examples of stem sentences from the Enigma Maths Hub. For example:

- To compare two-digit numbers, we need to compare the tens digits; if the tens digits are the same, we need to compare the ones digits.
- If the minuend and the subtrahend are changed by the same amount, the difference remains the same.

Staff explore how to use these sentences in context, and the importance of modelling these stems during lessons. Teachers work collaboratively to source, write and practise using the sentence stems to ensure they are confident in guiding pupils to use them independently.

In group work, pupils are encouraged to use the sentence stems to articulate their thinking with their peers. Working in pairs or small groups, they use stems to clarify their understanding, explain their reasoning and listen actively to each other. The sentence stems act as bridges between concrete understanding and abstract reasoning, providing pupils with the structure to explain their thoughts without being limited by their language proficiency.

At the end of the term, Sindi-Kate carries out lesson observations, reviews pupil work and holds discussions with staff to assess the effectiveness of the approach. There is a marked improvement in the quality of mathematical discussion in the classroom. Pupils who previously struggled to explain their thinking are more likely to volunteer to articulate their reasoning.

Leading reasoning across the school

Building a reasoning-rich school environment begins with equipping staff with the tools and confidence to embed reasoning into every lesson. Teachers must see reasoning not as an add-on but as a central part of teaching maths.

Monitoring reasoning

You will need to monitor the teaching and learning of reasoning to ensure it is consistently embedded across the school. When conducting learning walks or lesson drop-ins, focus on how reasoning is being modelled by the teachers and experienced by the pupils. Consider how open-ended tasks are used and how teachers narrate their thought processes. Look for common areas for development to feed into your plans for PD and coach staff individually to enhance particular aspects of their teaching.

When looking at pupils' books, consider what you want to get out of it. Books on their own don't offer an awful lot, so it might be helpful to sit alongside the teachers who can give context to the learning journey. Finding time for book looks alongside teachers can be tough, so you might be able to make it part of a staff training session, or ask your SLT if teachers can be released for 20 minute slots during your maths leadership time to discuss reasoning alongside their books. When you have time to conduct pupil voice, ask them to bring their books along so they can talk you through what they did and to gain an understanding of how they experience reasoning in their maths lessons.

Questions for reflection

- How can we support our teachers to integrate reasoning into daily lessons confidently?
- What feedback mechanisms can we put in place to ensure reasoning remains a focus in teaching and learning?
- How well does our school support all pupils, including those with SEND and those who are learning EAL, to engage in reasoning tasks?
- What structures can we put in place to share best practices and successes in reasoning across the school?

Example PD session: planning reasoning tasks

Here is an example of what a PD session on planning reasoning tasks could look like.

TIMING SUGGESTION	SESSION GUIDANCE

15 mins	• Think-Pair-Share: What do you understand by reasoning in maths? What does reasoning look like in your classroom? Do you think all pupils reason in your lessons? Why or why not?
	• Introduce key components of reasoning:
	  • making conjectures – forming ideas based on patterns
	  • justifying answers – explaining why something is true or false
	  • using logical steps – proving ideas with clear reasoning.
	• Discuss Nunes et al. (2009): reasoning is the biggest factor in success in maths – so it needs to be prioritised!

15 mins	• Watch a short clip (or enact a model of it if you can't video someone) of a teacher reasoning aloud using sentence stems like:
	  • 'I notice that…'
	  • 'This reminds me of…'
	  • 'I think this because…'
	• Ask teachers to work in pairs and discuss how they currently use mathematical talk in their lessons.
	• Plan a discussion-based reasoning question for an upcoming lesson using:
	  • 'odd one out' (Which number doesn't belong? Why?)
	  • 'true or false' (Is this always, sometimes, or never true?)
	  • 'what do you notice?' (Compare two representations of the same concept).

TIMING SUGGESTION	SESSION GUIDANCE

10 mins	• Present two types of question:
	  ◦ A closed question with one answer (What is 36 ÷ 4?).
	  ◦ A mathematically-rich task with reasoning opportunities (Find three different ways to divide 36 into equal groups. What do you notice?).
	• Discuss which question provides a richer mathematical experience and why.
	• Discuss what responses you would expect.
	• In small groups, teachers rewrite a question from an upcoming lesson to make it more reasoning-focused.

10 mins	• Show an incorrect solution to a problem and ask: What mistake was made? Why might the pupil have thought this was correct? How can we use this mistake to deepen understanding?
	• Teachers discuss how they respond to mistakes in their lessons. Do they:
	  ◦ celebrate them as learning opportunities
	  ◦ encourage pupils to explain errors
	  ◦ use them to clarify misconceptions?
	• Discuss the potential of a classroom routine where pupils respond to each other's answers, e.g. agreeing with, disagreeing with or building on a peer's response.

10 mins	• Ask teachers to sort reasoning tasks into those appropriate for:
	  ◦ EYFS – verbal reasoning, noticing patterns, sorting and classifying
	  ◦ KS1 – explaining number relationships and using pictures to justify answers
	  ◦ LKS2 – justifying calculations and comparing different methods
	  ◦ UKS2 – proving generalisations and algebraic reasoning.
	• Discuss whether the current practice in school is developing reasoning systematically. Where are the gaps?
	• Ask each teacher to choose a new reasoning strategy to implement next week.

After the session	• Work on a reasoning progression map to outline how reasoning develops across year groups. • Conduct informal learning walks to monitor reasoning strategies in action. • Gather pupil voice – do pupils feel confident reasoning in maths?

Explore further

- *Teaching for Mastery* (2019) by Mark McCourt
- The NCETM's article The Five Big Ideas at Primary – Mathematical Thinking (2025) by Dr Debbie Morgan: https://www.ncetm.org.uk/features/the-five-big-ideas-at-primary-mathematical-thinking/
- The chapter 'Reasoning' in *Thinking Deeply about Primary Mathematics* (2020) by Kieran Mackle

Chapter summary

- Mathematical reasoning involves finding patterns and connections, making generalisations and justifying answers.
- It promotes deeper understanding, critical thinking and connections between mathematical concepts.
- We can scaffold reasoning by providing sentence stems and model how to use these.
- Reasoning starts with exploratory talk in EYFS and progresses to formal arguments in UKS2.
- Reasoning is for all pupils. Teachers can use scaffolds for pupils with SEND and those who are learning English as an additional language.
- Maths leaders should create a reasoning culture by training staff, providing resources and monitoring its integration into lessons.

7 Problem solving

Problem solving is at the core of mathematical thinking and connects fluency and reasoning. It encourages pupils to explore, make decisions and apply their knowledge in meaningful contexts. As an often misunderstood and mis-taught aspect of the primary maths curriculum, it is important that subject leaders have a clear sense of direction when working on problem solving. In Ofsted's mathematics subject report, they found that 'Curriculum decisions about problem solving are often left to individual class teachers' (2023). This chapter will look at the role of problem solving in primary maths, the benefits of problem solving and how to get everyone involved in problem solving.

The role of problem solving in primary maths

Problem solving is more than just an activity within maths lessons. It is a fundamental approach to learning that helps pupils make connections and think outside of the box in all areas of life. When problem solving is embedded effectively in the curriculum, it fosters deeper understanding, develops metacognition and demonstrates the real-world relevance of maths. We should avoid tokenistic problem solving such as 'Problem-Solving Fridays' or problem-solving challenge questions for greater depth pupils. It should be woven into the fabric of our maths curriculum.

Connecting concepts

Maths is not a collection of isolated skills but a web of interconnected ideas. Problem solving allows pupils to see how different areas of maths link together, strengthening their understanding and recall. For example, a problem involving perimeter and area will likely require knowledge of multiplication, addition and spatial reasoning. Similarly, a data-handling task will require knowledge of the four operations.

When pupils experience maths in this interconnected way, they are more likely to transfer skills between topics and retain their learning. This approach also prevents the fragmented learning that can occur when mathematical concepts are taught in isolation. A pupil who understands the relationship between fractions, decimals and percentages through problem-solving contexts will be better equipped to use them in real-life situations.

Developing metacognition

Metacognition – the ability to think about one's own thinking – can be developed through problem solving. Pupils who reflect on their strategies, evaluate their approaches and learn from mistakes become more independent and resilient learners. Encouraging metacognitive thinking in problem solving can be done through structured questioning and self-reflection. By verbalising their thought processes, pupils develop a deeper awareness of how they solve problems and become better equipped to adapt their methods in future tasks. Teachers can prompt pupils by asking targeted questions. For example:

- What strategy did you choose and why?
- What worked well in your approach?
- What would you do differently next time?

One effective strategy is to model metacognition through teacher-led worked examples. By thinking aloud while solving a problem, teachers can highlight decisions, identify potential mistakes and adjust the approach, which demonstrates how expert problem solvers reflect on their thinking.

In practice: a teacher-led worked example

For example, if the problem is 'Ben spent some of his birthday money. He gave £3 to his sister, then bought a book for £6.50. After that, he had £4.50 left. How much birthday money did he start with?' The teacher's thinking aloud might look like this:

WHAT THE TEACHER SAYS	WHAT THE TEACHER DRAWS/ WRITES
'Let's read the question carefully first. Ben gave £3 to his sister, then spent £6.50 on a book, and had £4.50 left after that. The question is asking how much money he started with. So, I don't need to go forwards – I need to work backwards from what he has left.'	

'I know that he ended up with £4.50. This bar represents the money he was left with.'	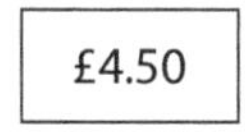
'I know that just before he ended with £4.50, he bought a book for £6.50. I can work out that before he bought the book, he must have had £6.50 more than the £4.50 he was left with. The next part of the bar represents the £6.50 he spent on a book.'	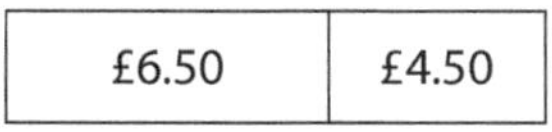
'So, I'll do £4.50 + £6.50. That's £11.00. I'll double-check: £4 + £6 = £10, and 50p + 50p = £1. So that makes £11.'	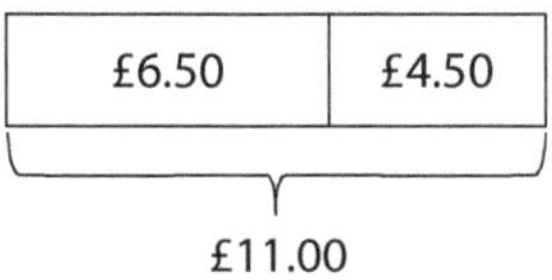
'Now I know that he had £11 before he bought the book. I also know that he gave £3 to his sister before that. So, to find out how much he had at the very beginning, I need to add that £3 back on. I'll draw another part of the bar to represent the £3.'	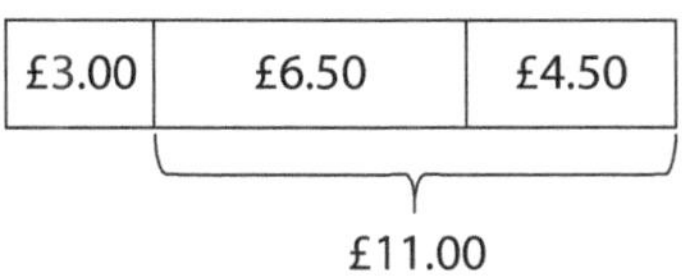
'So now I can add £11 and £3. I know 11 + 3 = 14, so that means Ben started with £14.'	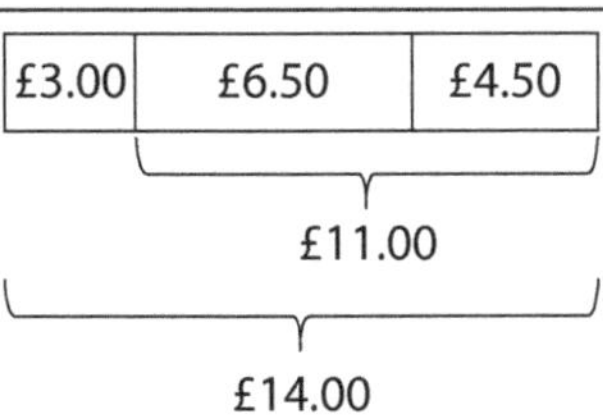
'Let me just check the whole sequence forwards to be sure: I start with £14. Take away £3 to give to his sister, which is £11. Take away £6.50 for the book, so there is £4.50 left.'	

Additionally, peer discussion can help reinforce metacognitive skills. When pupils explain their reasoning to others, they refine their understanding and are exposed to alternative strategies. Encouraging classroom discussions where pupils compare different approaches fosters a culture where thinking processes are valued as much as correct answers.

Making maths relevant

Problem solving can not only develop mathematical skills but also build problem-solving strategies that pupils can carry into adulthood. They also help answer the common question 'Why do we need to learn this?' by showing the role of maths in decision making, financial literacy and problem solving in various careers. As a maths leader, you can support staff by curating a bank of real-world problem-solving activities and writing these into the curriculum, even if you use a bought-in scheme of work. This doesn't need to be a big job – you could set aside some time in a PD session on problem solving for staff to brainstorm or source examples of real-world maths problems. Often, some of the best work comes from involving your colleagues and collaborating across phases. You can also promote collaboration across subjects, working with science, geography or DT leads to embed problem-solving tasks in different contexts.

Real-world problem-solving tasks give pupils opportunities to apply their mathematical knowledge in meaningful contexts that span curriculum areas. Examples include:

- planning a budget: pupils calculate costs for a class event, considering prices, discounts and total expenditure
- interpreting data: pupils analyse real-life statistics, such as climate data or sports scores, to draw conclusions and make predictions
- creating a product: pupils can design a product and its packaging, create the net with suitable dimensions, source equipment or ingredients and work out how to price their product to sell at a school fair or event
- planning a trip: pupils plan a class trip, working out distances, travel times, ticket prices, group discounts and timetables
- designing a school garden: pupils plan the layout of a garden space, calculate area and perimeter, consider planting ratios and budget for seeds and equipment

- organising a sports day: pupils create a timetable, calculate scoring systems, track class/team points using tally charts and graphs and work out averages or rankings
- energy usage audit: pupils collect data from around the school about electricity usage, for example lightbulbs per room and devices used, then calculate totals and suggest cost-saving measures using unit rates and bar charts.

Types of maths problems

Broadly, problem solving tasks can be categorised into routine problems, non-routine problems and investigations. Whether a problem is routine or non-routine isn't always obvious in the way it has been written. It also depends on whether or not the pupil has had experience of that type of problem. If they have worked on problems of that type before, it becomes more routine. However, a seemingly straightforward and routine problem to us as adults will be less obvious for the pupils.

Routine problems

Routine problems are problems that pupils can solve using a procedure or method that they have already learnt, often involving arithmetic, algebra or ratio. Pupils can see a way of solving the problem and then calculate. Routine problems are not always closed problems (problems with a single, definitive answer), but they can be. They are more straightforward because they have a clear pathway to finding the solution.

In practice: example routine problems

EYFS:

- You have 3 apples and get 2 more. How many do you have now?
- Show me 6 using two different Numicon pieces.
- What number comes after 4?

KS1:

- What is 12 + 8?
- What is double 7?
- A pencil costs 15p and a rubber costs 5p. How much do they cost altogether?

LKS2:
- What is 346 + 275?
- What is 63 ÷ 7?
- What is $\frac{1}{3}$ of 21?

UKS2:
- A rectangle has a length of 8cm and a width of 3cm. What is its area?
- What fraction of 20 is 5?
- What is 12% of 250?

These problems are important for practising fluency in different contexts as they allow pupils to strengthen their recall of methods and procedures. They also build confidence in handling calculations, ensuring that pupils have a solid foundation before moving on to more complex problem types.

Non-routine problems

Non-routine problems require pupils to think critically, as the pupils do not have an immediate way to solve them. These problems may have multiple approaches or require pupils to select an appropriate strategy rather than following a memorised procedure.

In practice: example non-routine problems

EYFS:
- I have 5 counters. Some are red, and some are blue. How many could be red?
- Can you find two numbers that add to 10 but aren't the same?

KS1:
- You have 20p. What different combinations of coins could you use?
- There are 12 legs in the field. How many animals could there be if they are ducks and cows?
- Use 3, 4 and 5 to make a number sentence.

LKS2:
- Arrange these digits to make the largest possible odd number: 3, 7, 2, 9, 1.
- What is the missing number in this pattern? 2, 6, 12, 20, __, 42.
- I'm thinking of a number. When I double it and subtract 5, I get 27. What is my number?

UKS2:

- A farmer has chickens and cows. There are 20 heads and 48 legs altogether. How many of each animal are there, not including the farmer?
- I'm thinking of a number. If I divide it by 3 and then add 7, I get 22. What's the number?
- The perimeter of a rectangle is 36cm. One side is 4cm longer than the other. What are the side lengths?

These problems develop problem-solving resilience and require pupils to make connections between different areas of maths. They also promote mathematical discussion, as pupils explain and justify their thinking.

Mathematical investigations

Investigations go beyond single-answer problem solving by encouraging pupils to explore mathematical ideas, make generalisations and test theories (Dabell, 2025). Investigations promote deep mathematical thinking and wider exploration of a topic. These are examples of investigations:

- Exploring number patterns: What happens when you add consecutive numbers?
- Shape and space investigations: How many different nets can be made for a cube?
- Generalisation tasks: If I multiply any two odd numbers, what kind of number do I always get? Can I prove it?

Investigations require pupils to think like mathematicians by posing questions, testing ideas, refining methods and drawing conclusions. They develop problem-solving stamina and mathematical curiosity, and allow pupils to see the creativity and exploration within maths.

Case study: introducing non-linear problems into the curriculum

Genevieve, a passionate maths leader at Greenfield Primary School, identifies a gap in her school's approach to problem solving. Although her team is proficient in teaching basic arithmetic and routine problem solving, pupils are struggling with non-routine problems that require creative, critical thinking rather than just applying a set procedure. Recognising that these problems foster deeper understanding and help pupils build resilience, she decides to introduce more non-routine problems into the curriculum.

To begin, Genevieve reviews the school's existing problem-solving strategies and notices that, while pupils are often asked to solve problems, there are few opportunities for them to tackle complex, multi-step problems that require diverse strategies. Non-routine problems that demand critical thinking are almost entirely absent. Genevieve wants to ensure that her pupils can engage in meaningful problem-solving experiences that not only build mathematical skills but also cultivate curiosity and perseverance.

Genevieve starts by researching the types of non-routine problems that are suitable for primary school pupils. She had heard her old maths lead talk about NRICH for problem solving, so she heads to the NRICH website to look at the variety of problems that they have. She focuses on problems that involve reasoning and multiple steps, such as puzzles, logic problems and real-world scenarios. Next, Genevieve works with her teaching team to integrate these types of problems into daily lessons. She emphasises that non-routine problems should be approached differently from routine ones. Genevieve encourages teachers to model various strategies to solve non-routine problems, such as trial and improvement, working backwards, working systematically and finding patterns. She also leads PD sessions on how to guide pupils through these problems, focusing on the importance of explaining their thinking and reflecting on their strategies.

To make these problems accessible to all pupils, Genevieve ensures that they are scaffolded appropriately. She is released once a half-term to work alongside a different year group, supporting her colleagues to create a series of supporting resources, such as step-by-step guides, visuals like bar models and hints to break down complex problems into smaller, manageable parts. These scaffolds help pupils, particularly those with SEND or who are learning EAL, engage with the problems without feeling overwhelmed. To help pupils reflect on their thought processes, teachers are also encouraged to ask metacognitive questions such as, 'What do you know so far?' and 'What strategy might work here?'

As non-linear problems become a regular part of lessons, Genevieve observes a significant shift in her pupils' problem-solving abilities. They are more confident in tackling unfamiliar problems, more resilient in the face of challenge and better able to explain and justify their reasoning. The collaborative approach, where pupils work together and share strategies, also fosters a supportive learning environment.

At the end of the academic year, Genevieve conducts a review of the impact of these changes. Through book looks, pupil discussions and assessments, she finds that pupils are demonstrating stronger problem-solving skills, particularly in tasks that require creative thinking and multiple steps. This success is largely attributed to consistent exposure to non-linear problems, the support provided by teachers and the focus on metacognition and reflection.

Supporting all pupils in problem solving

All pupils, regardless of 'ability' or background, should have access to high-quality opportunities for problem solving because it is an important part of mathematical development. However, pupils will have different levels of confidence, experience and skill when tackling problem-solving tasks. Highly effective teaching ensures that all pupils, including those with SEND, EAL pupils and pupils who have previously worked above expectations, can access problem solving in a meaningful way. It is your role as the maths leader to champion the inclusion of all pupils in problem-solving lessons.

Pupils with SEND

Pupils with SEND may face additional challenges in problem solving, such as difficulties with working memory, processing speed or language comprehension. To support them effectively, teachers should focus on reducing cognitive load and providing alternative ways to engage with mathematical problems. As the maths lead, consider how you could lead from the front and create an in-house set of principles for ensuring that all pupils can access problem solving. Ideas for scaffolding problem solving could include the following strategies.

Breaking problems into manageable steps and using visual aids

Multi-step problems can feel overwhelming for some pupils with SEND, so breaking them into a sequence of smaller, structured steps can help. Teachers might use guided questioning or structured prompts, such as:

- What do we know?
- What are we trying to find out?
- What strategy could we use?

One of the most effective ways to make problem solving more accessible is to reduce complexity without removing challenge. This can involve simplifying the language of the problem, breaking it into shorter sentences or using symbols and pictures to reinforce meaning. Providing concrete manipulatives, such as counters, number lines and bar models helps pupils to visualise problems and develop their reasoning.

In practice: broken-down problem

Original problem:

A shopkeeper has 135 apples. She puts them into bags with 9 apples in each. She sells 7 of the bags. How many apples does she have left?

As with many worded questions, there's multiple pieces of information in one sentence, it requires multiple steps, there's no structured support and the language is quite abstract.

Broken-down problem:

1. The shopkeeper has 135 apples.
2. She puts 9 apples into each bag.
3. How many bags does she make?
4. She sells 7 bags.
5. How many bags are left?
6. How many apples are left in those bags?

This problem has been broken down into simpler sentences. These steps can be revealed one at a time so that pupils can focus their attention on the new step each time. You could scaffold pupils' responses with the structure 'First... Then... Now... Next... Now... So...' For example 'First, she has 135 apples. Then, she puts 9 apples into each bag. Now she has ? bags of apples. Next, she sells 7 bags of apples. Now, she has ? bags of apples left. So, she has ? apples left.' Base 10 can be used to represent the apples.

Alternative methods of expression

Not all pupils can easily articulate their thinking in writing. Allowing pupils to use alternative methods such as drawing, demonstrating with manipulatives or explaining their thinking to a partner enables them to demonstrate their understanding in ways that suit their needs. It's a good idea to encourage teachers to model utilising different strategies with their pupils so that they feel comfortable trying out different strategies for jotting down their thinking. Then when pupils are confident expressing their thoughts in the way that makes sense to them, teachers can show different examples under the visualiser for their peers to discuss.

EAL pupils

For pupils learning EAL, the language of problem solving can be a significant barrier. Even if they have strong mathematical understanding, unfamiliar vocabulary or complex sentence structures can prevent them from fully engaging with a problem. Using vocabulary banks that include key problem-solving terms (such as 'more than', 'fewer', 'altogether', 'total' and 'difference') can help pupils navigate word problems with greater confidence. These should be accessible for the pupils and reinforced regularly. Dual-language resources, where appropriate, can also help pupils learning EAL make connections between their first language and English.

Pupils working above expectations

Pupils who have previously worked above expectations may grasp problem-solving techniques quickly, but they still need challenge and opportunities for deeper thinking. Simply giving them more problems to solve at the same level is unlikely to extend their learning. These pupils may benefit from problems that require them to explore multiple strategies, make generalisations or justify their reasoning. Questions such as 'Can you find another way?', 'Is this always true?' and 'How many solutions are there?' will encourage deeper mathematical thinking.

Assessing problem solving

Assessing problem solving goes beyond simply checking whether pupils arrive at the correct answer – it must also be about evaluating their process, reasoning and ability to apply strategies effectively.

Process vs. outcome

Encourage teachers to assess the reasoning and strategies pupils use, rather than focusing solely on accuracy. A pupil who arrives at the correct answer without understanding the method is not truly developing problem-solving skills. Conversely, a pupil who makes a mistake but demonstrates clear reasoning and a sound approach is making important progress. Consider asking questions in assessments that require pupils to explain their thinking, such as:

- Can you demonstrate another way to solve this?
- Why did you choose this method?
- What would you do differently next time?
- Was this the most efficient method?

Providing teachers with guidance on assessing process over product as above can help shift the focus from pure correctness to deeper mathematical thinking, which will in turn impact the culture of maths teaching and learning in the school.

Creating assessment opportunities

As the maths lead, think about your maths curriculum and if it is testing problem solving. It is likely that there might be some problem-solving-style questions within your curriculum, but these are often an afterthought or the last task on a long set of independent questions that only the fastest pupils get to. You could look into one phase per term to get a good idea of what sort of problems are already in the curriculum. If you can get support from colleagues within that phase who are keen to get involved in shaping the curriculum, this will be much faster and you will have people to bounce ideas around with.

Work alongside your teaching colleagues to identify key moments for problem solving in your curriculum and to ensure a balance of routine and non-routine problems and investigations. If problem solving is a key focus for your school, it is worth spending a PD meeting looking at a particular strand of the curriculum, for example addition and subtraction; look at when pupils are likely to be in a place where they can use what they have learned to solve a longer problem, rather than doing more and more fluency. It is also worth spending time considering which strategies the problems within your curriculum require so that there is a mix of working systematically, working backwards, trial and improvement and finding patterns.

Monitoring problem solving

As a maths lead, one of your key responsibilities is to ensure that problem solving is not just included in the curriculum but is also embedded effectively and consistently across all year groups. To do this, you need to evaluate the impact of how problem solving is being taught and how pupils are engaging with it.

Learning walks and pupil voice

One of the most effective ways to monitor problem solving is through classroom observations during learning walks and discussions with pupils. When visiting lessons, pay close attention to how pupils articulate their strategies and justify their reasoning, whether teachers are prompting discussion through open-ended questions, and the use of collaborative problem solving.

Pupil voice is another valuable tool. Speak to pupils about how they approach problem solving. Ask them what they do when they feel stuck, whether they can explain their thinking and if they can identify other ways to solve a problem. The way pupils respond will give you some insight into whether problem-solving skills are being effectively taught and embedded. It will also support you to look at how the curriculum has been organised and how problem solving has been woven into the sequence of learning.

Book looks

Looking at pupils' exercise books and workbooks can also provide useful evidence of how problem solving is being developed across the school, but it isn't enough just to look at books and written work. When reviewing work, consider whether it would be more beneficial to do this alongside the pupils to gain their insights or alongside the teachers to provide context for the work. Look for evidence of methods and structured working out, a logical progression in problem-solving steps and opportunities for reflection. Do pupils evaluate their strategies or justify their choices? Encouraging teachers to build reflection into problem-solving tasks, such as asking pupils to provide short explanations of how they solved a problem or what they learned from it, can deepen understanding and provide further assessment opportunities.

Your role is to ensure that monitoring of problem solving is a meaningful and actionable task. If you work with staff to develop consistent approaches, then the pupils' experience of problem solving will improve. Consider how you can provide PD on effective questioning techniques, assessing process vs. outcome and using pupil discussions to gauge understanding. By embedding these assessment strategies into everyday teaching, and monitoring their impact, you can ensure that problem solving is not just an occasional activity but a key part of mathematical learning across your school.

Questions for reflection

- How is problem solving currently embedded in maths teaching across our school?
- Do teachers feel confident teaching problem solving? What PD or resources could support them?
- How do we ensure problem solving is accessible to all pupils, including those with SEND and those learning EAL?
- Does our school have a clear progression of problem-solving strategies from EYFS to Year 6?
- How do we assess and monitor problem solving in our school? Are we focusing on both process and outcome?

Example PD session: using problem-solving strategies

Here is an example of what a PD session on using problem-solving strategies could look like.

<table>
<tr><th>TIMING SUGGESTION</th><th>SESSION GUIDANCE</th></tr>
<tr><td>5 mins</td><td>

- Discuss what makes a good problem solver.
- Ask teachers to reflect on these questions:
  - Do my pupils struggle to start solving problems?
  - Do they rely too much on guessing rather than strategy?
  - Do they often give up when a problem seems difficult?

</td></tr>
<tr><td>20 mins</td><td>

- Go through four core problem-solving strategies with clear worked examples. Model solving each problem and narrating your thinking along the way. Teachers to follow along, solving problems step-by-step as each strategy is modelled.
- Strategy 1: Working systematically
  - What it means: listing all possibilities in an organised way.
  - Example: How many different ways can you arrange the letters A, B, and C?
- Strategy 2: Working backwards
  - What it means: starting with the solution and reversing the steps.
  - Example: Find a number between 1 and 100 that, when doubled and added to 12, equals 98.
- Strategy 3: Trial and improvement
  - What it means: making an informed guess, checking and then refining.
  - Example: _ _ _ _ _ x 3 = _ _ _ _ _ The missing numbers in this equation use the digits 0-9 once each. Replace the blank spaces with the digits.
- Strategy 4: Finding patterns
  - What it means: looking for sequences, relationships, or rules.
  - Example: What is the next number in the sequence 2, 6, 12, 20, __, 42?

</td></tr>
</table>

TIMING SUGGESTION	SESSION GUIDANCE

15 mins	• Each group is given one problem, but each teacher must solve it using two different strategies. Teachers work through a problem using different strategies.
	• Whole-group reflection:
	  • Which strategy was easier?
	  • Would pupils be able to apply this independently?
	  • How can we help pupils choose the best strategy for a given problem?

15 mins	• Share a collection of problems and have the teachers sort them into appropriate phases. • Ask them to write down what pre-requisite knowledge is needed to solve each problem. • Then, ask them to consider how to scaffold the problem solving. Choose one problem to focus on and design a lesson around it.

5 mins	• Quick audit: Teachers reflect on their own practice:
	  • Do I explicitly teach problem-solving strategies?
	  • Do my pupils use a range of approaches?
	  • How do I assess problem solving beyond correct answers?
	• Action step: Each teacher commits to focusing on one strategy in their teaching next week.

After the session	• Support teachers in explicitly modelling strategies by team teaching or putting on demo lessons. • Monitor reasoning in problem solving through learning walks, book looks and pupil discussions. • Create a bank of rich problem-solving tasks for routine and non-routine problems.

Explore further

- *How to Solve It* (2004) by George Pólya
- EEF's blog *The Problem with Problem-Solving in Maths* (2021) by Kirstin Mulholland: https://educationendowmentfoundation.org.uk/news/eef-blog-the-problem-with-problem-solving-in-maths
- Third Space Learning's blog *Maths Problem Solving: Engaging your Students and Strengthening their Mathematical Skills* (2025) by Meriel Willatt: https://thirdspacelearning.com/blog/maths-problem-solving/

Chapter summary

- Problem solving should be embedded across the curriculum rather than a one-off activity so that pupils make connections, develop metacognitive strategies and apply their learning meaningfully.
- Teachers should understand that there are routine, non-routine and investigative problems, ensuring pupils experience a broad range of challenges that encourage both procedural fluency and critical thinking.
- All pupils, including those with SEND, learning EAL or working below the age-related expectation, must have meaningful access to problem solving through strategies like scaffolding, alternative ways of recording, vocabulary support and low-threshold/high-ceiling tasks.
- Assessment should go beyond correct answers and consider the processes pupils use, with opportunities to explain strategies, reflect on their thinking and demonstrate understanding in varied ways.
- Subject leaders should monitor problem solving through book looks, learning walks and pupil voice to evaluate impact, guide professional development, and ensure consistent, high-quality provision across the school.

8 Models, manipulatives and structures

Models are representations that help pupils understand abstract concepts by making the underlying structures more visible. Manipulatives are physical objects, such as counters and Dienes, that pupils can handle to explore and demonstrate mathematical thinking. Structures refer to the consistent patterns and relationships that underpin mathematical operations and concepts. This chapter explores how models and manipulatives can support conceptual understanding, the arithmetic structures that primary pupils need to understand and the importance of systematic and consistent introduction across the school. It will also offer guidance on how maths leaders can monitor and support their use effectively.

Models and manipulatives, including the concrete-pictorial-abstract model

Mathematical models and representations are integral in helping pupils to develop conceptual understanding. They provide tangible ways to explore abstract mathematical concepts. For example, using a place value chart to understand how numbers are made of digits that hold a value based on their position within the number. Research suggests that pupils who use a variety of representations develop greater mathematical flexibility (Nunes et al., 2009).

Sweller's Cognitive Load Theory explains how the brain processes and retains new information (1988). According to Sweller, our working memory is limited, meaning pupils can struggle when presented with too much abstract information at once. Effective models and representations help to reduce cognitive load by breaking complex mathematical concepts into manageable steps.

The concrete-pictorial-abstract (CPA) model

The CPA model is a prominent feature of effective maths teaching. It is important for you to understand the CPA model because it underpins how children build a deep and transferable understanding of mathematical concepts.

By understanding how a child might be introduced to a concept with a concrete manipulative first and how powerful pictorial representations can be, you can support staff to use CPA effectively in their lessons. Table 2 on the next page shows some examples of how concrete, pictorial and abstract representations can be used in primary maths.

Concrete

Concrete representations, sometimes referred to as manipulatives, include counters, cubes, number rods and other resources that pupils can physically handle to explore mathematical concepts and structures. When introducing a new concept, giving pupils the chance to build an understanding while they can physically touch and move the manipulatives might mean that they can see the maths more than if it were introduced abstractly first. Findings from Carbonneau et al. (2013) show that concrete manipulatives:

- can have moderate to large effects in retention
- are most effective when there is clear instruction to link abstract or complex concepts to the concrete representation
- benefit pupils with low prior knowledge so that they can 'see' the maths rather than just 'do' the maths.

Pictorial

Pictorial representations include images of concrete manipulatives, diagrams and specific visuals used in maths, such as number lines and bar models. Pictorial representations make connections between concrete resources and number sentences or written methods. Enabling pupils to be able to visualise a problem is a key benefit of using pictorial representations.

Abstract

Abstract representations refer to the use of number sentences and written calculation. If teachers begin with abstract representations without first giving pupils enough exposure to the underlying mathematical structures using concrete and pictorial representations, pupils may end up memorising procedures without truly understanding them. For example, if pupils are taught the column method for subtraction before exploring the concept of exchanging with place value counters or Dienes, they might carry out the steps correctly but have no conceptual idea as to why they are exchanging a ten.

Table 2 Concrete, pictorial and abstract examples

PHASE	CONTENT	REPRESENTATIONS		
		CONCRETE	**PICTORIAL**	**ABSTRACT**
EYFS	Recognising the number three	Counting the counters in a ten frame 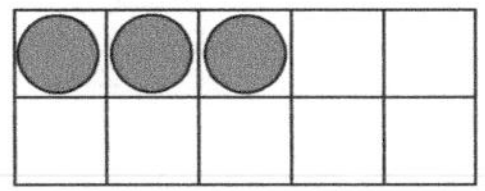 **Figure 8.1** Three counters in a ten-frame	Drawing counters on a ten frame 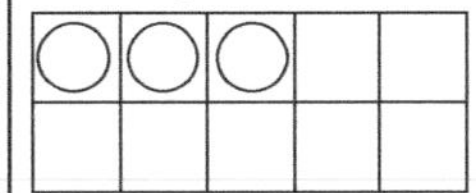 **Figure 8.2** Three circles drawn in a ten-frame to represent counters	**3** Recognising the numeral for three
KS1	Bridging to ten to add numbers within 20: 7 + 5	Laying counters on ten frames to make ten first 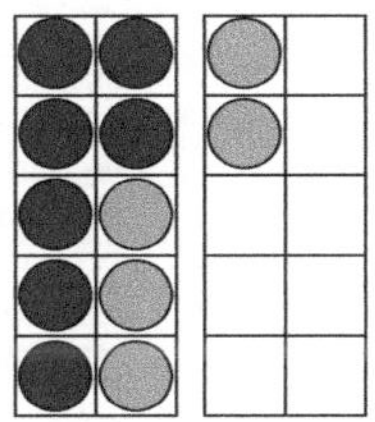 **Figure 8.3** Seven black and five white counters in two ten-frames to show 7 + 5 = 7 + 3 + 2	Making ten on a number line and then adding the rest 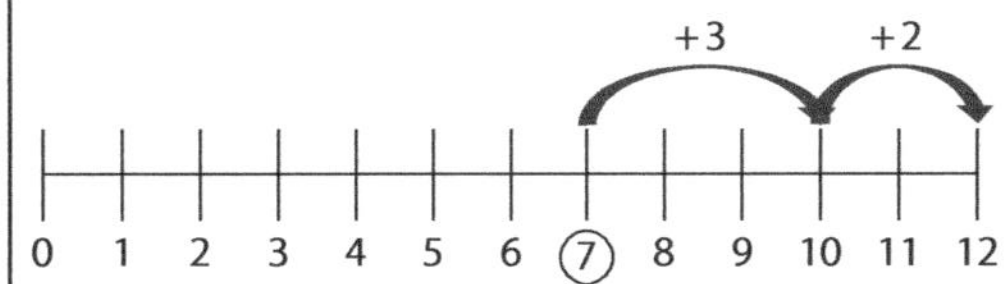 **Figure 8.4** 1–12 number line showing 7 + 5 = 7 + 3 + 2	7 + 5 = 7 + 3 + 2 (5 partitioned into 3 and 2) Making ten by partitioning one addend
KS2	Column addition: 238 + 149	Using Dienes to lay out addition in columns 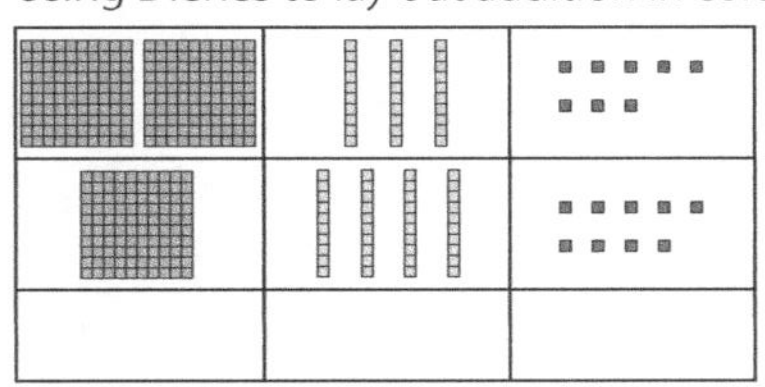 **Figure 8.5** Dienes in place-value columns, showing 238 and 149	Sketching Dienes and making jottings in columns 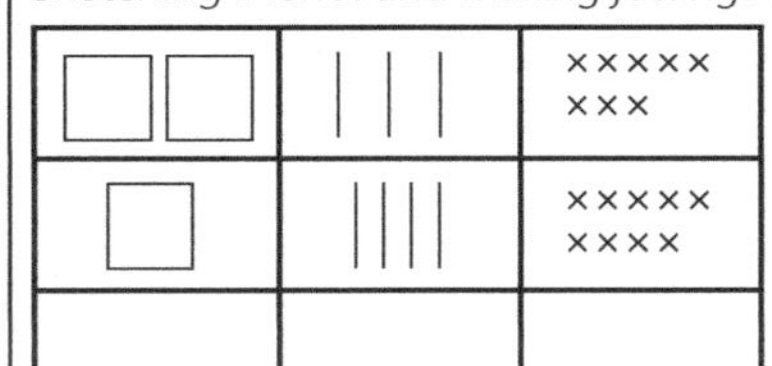 **Figure 8.6** Hand-drawn representations of Dienes in place-value columns, showing 238 and 149	Laying out digits in column method

It is important to stress that this is not to say that concrete, pictorial and abstract is a linear sequence. Introducing the abstract representation alongside the concrete or pictorial representations can lead to strong links between pupils' conceptual understanding and procedural knowledge.

The importance of arithmetic structure

One of the NCETM's five big ideas is 'representation and structure'. The inclusion of structure highlights the importance of using concrete and visual representations to expose arithmetic structures. Arithmetic structure refers to the underlying patterns and relationships linked to how numbers and operations work. It's about understanding what stays the same and what changes when we add, subtract, multiply or divide. Rather than seeing calculations as isolated procedures, arithmetic structure helps pupils recognise the consistent mathematical relationships and patterns beneath them.

Arithmetic structures are a sometimes-underused aspect of teaching primary maths, which can lead to pupils having an insecure understanding of what the four operations actually look like when broken down. Table 3 on pages 118–119 shows how we can use models and representations to show the arithmetic structures that Haylock (2024) describes in *Mathematics Explained for Primary Teachers*.

The beauty and power of using representations effectively lies in their ability to reveal the underlying structures of the maths at hand. For pupils to be successful, they need to learn to look beyond surface features and recognise the structure of a problem. This structural awareness begins with concrete and pictorial representations, which serve as bridges to abstract thinking. By physically manipulating concrete resources or visualising relationships through pictorial representations, pupils can grasp the deep structure of problems before they move to just using the abstract maths.

Systematic introduction of arithmetic structures

As a subject leader, you should have an oversight of how the structures of arithmetic are taught and understood in your school. It may be that you need to consider how to equip your colleagues with the relevant knowledge to teach this well and decide how best to communicate the arithmetic structures with your pupils.

Once the teachers are confident with arithmetic structures and how best to use models and representations, they will be able to tackle problems like problems A and B in class, and their pupils will be more able to draw out the problems and see the maths behind them.

Problem A: Greenfield Academy has 350 pupils. Brookside School has 95 pupils more than Greenfield Academy. Riverside Primary has 58 pupils more than Greenfield Academy. How many pupils are there altogether?

Problem B: The mass of a box is 120 kg more than a suitcase. The mass of a backpack is 90 kg less than the box. Altogether, the mass of the three items is 360 kg. What is the mass of the box?

Consistency and coherence across year groups

For models and representations to be effective, they must be used consistently across year groups. Consistent use of models and representations can be one of the most effective ways to build deep and sustained understanding for pupils. A lack of consistency can result in:

- pupils struggling with new representations because they have not been introduced explicitly or progressively. For example, if pupils encounter a number line for the first time when learning about fractions in KS2, they may find it difficult to interpret the representation, leading to confusion rather than clarity.
- misconceptions developing due to inconsistent explanations, terminology or application. For example, if one teacher refers to the 'whole' in a part-whole model while another calls it the 'total' or 'sum' without explanation, pupils may not make the connection between the two, weakening their understanding of number relationships and addition structure.
- teachers using different representations for the same concept without explaining how the representations are connected. For example, one teacher might use a bar model to represent multiplication as repeated addition, while another uses arrays without making any links between the two. If pupils aren't explicitly shown how the bar model and the array both represent the same mathematical structure, they may see them as unrelated strategies, missing the chance to build a connected understanding of multiplication.

Table 3 Models and representations to teach arithmetic structures

<table>
<tr><td rowspan="3">ADDITIVE: ADDITION</td><td colspan="3">Aggregation: combining two or more parts to find the sum</td><td colspan="3">Augmentation: increasing a quantity by a given amount</td></tr>
<tr><td colspan="3">There are 42 blue cars and 58 red cars in a car park.
How many are there in total?</td><td colspan="3">First, there are 42 cars in the car park. Then, 58 more cars arrive.
How many cars are there now?</td></tr>
<tr><td colspan="3">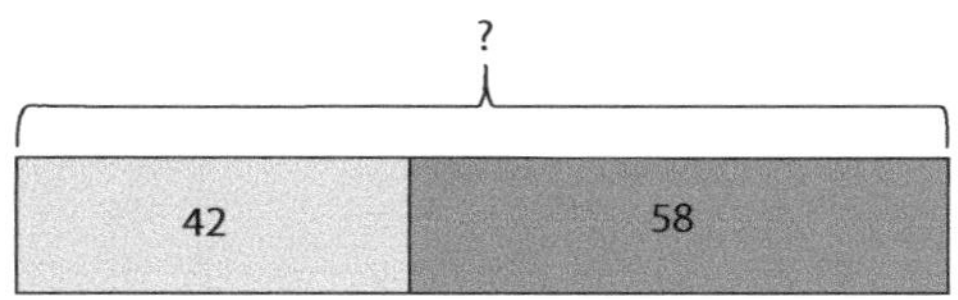

Figure 8.7 Bar model for 42 + 58 = ?</td><td colspan="3">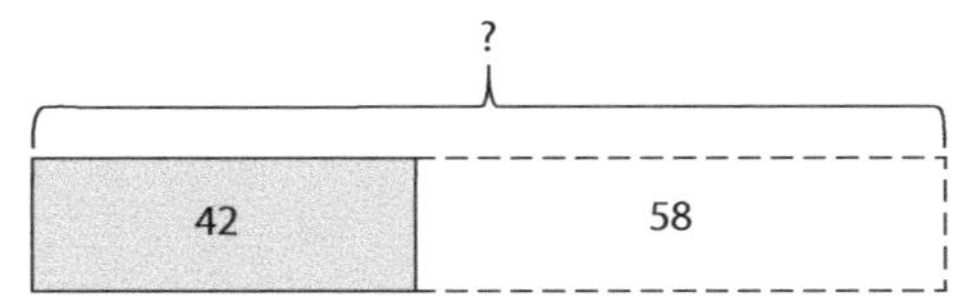

Figure 8.8 Bar model for 42 + 58 = ?</td></tr>
<tr><td rowspan="3">ADDITIVE: SUBTRACTION</td><td colspan="2">Reduction: taking away from the whole</td><td colspan="2">Partition: finding one part when you know the whole and the other part(s)</td><td colspan="2">Comparison: finding the difference between two quantities</td></tr>
<tr><td colspan="2">There are 100 cars in the car park.
42 drive out of the car park.
How many cars are left?</td><td colspan="2">There are 100 cars in the car park.
42 of them are red and the rest are blue.
How many cars are blue?</td><td colspan="2">There are 42 red cars and 58 blue cars in a car park.
How many more blue cars are there than red cars?</td></tr>
<tr><td colspan="2">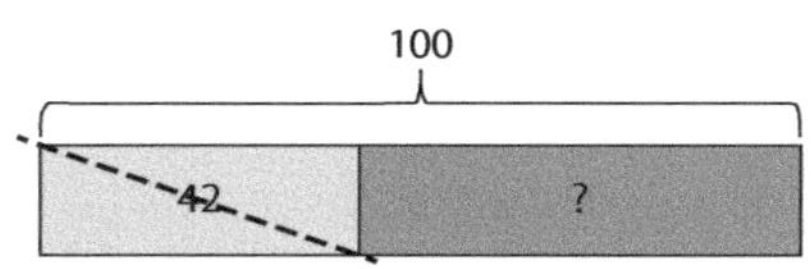

Figure 8.9 Bar model for 100 – 42 = ?</td><td colspan="2">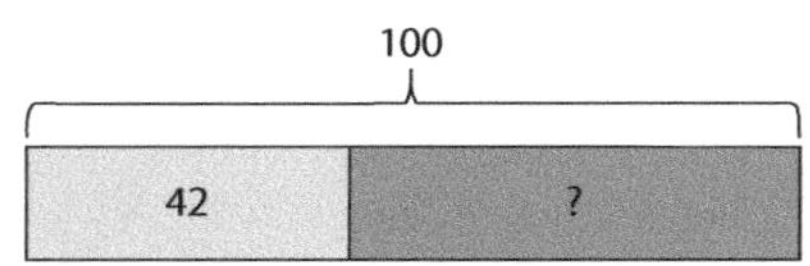

Figure 8.10 Bar model for 100 – 42 = ?</td><td colspan="2">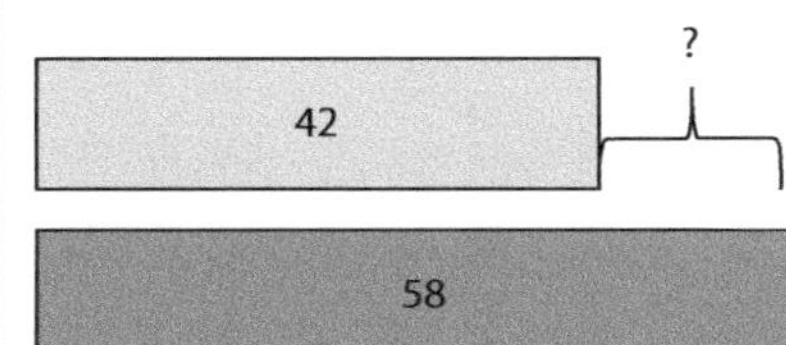

Figure 8.11 Comparison bar model for 58 – 42 = ?</td></tr>
</table>

MULTIPLICATIVE: MULTIPLICATION	**Repeated addition: adding equal groups**	**Scaling: increasing a quantity proportionally**
	There are four cookies in a box. There are 13 boxes. How many cookies are there in total?	An individual cookie uses 13 g of chocolate chips. A sharing cookie uses four times as many chocolate chips. What is the mass of the chocolate chips for a sharing cookie?
	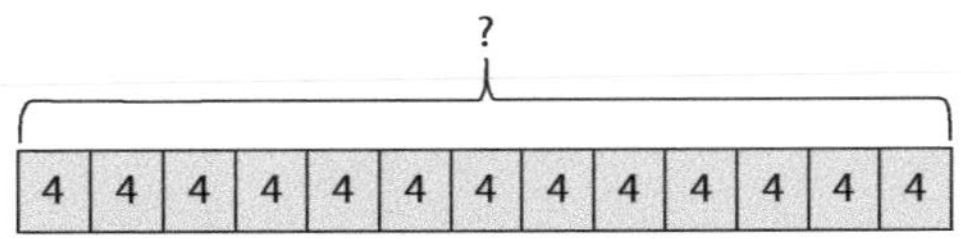 **Figure 8.12** Bar model for $13 \times 4 = ?$	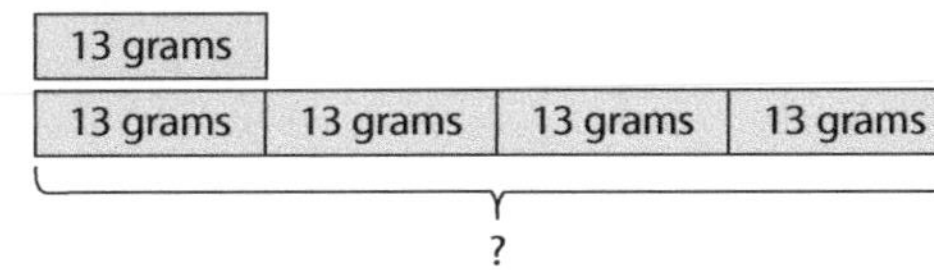 **Figure 8.13** Bar model for 4 lots of 13 grams
MULTIPLICATIVE: DIVISION	**Quotitive: splitting into groups of a given number**	**Partitive: sharing into a given number of groups**
	A baker bakes 32 cookies. She puts them into boxes of four cookies. How many boxes are there?	A baker cooks 32 cookies. She puts them into four boxes. How many cookies are in each box?
	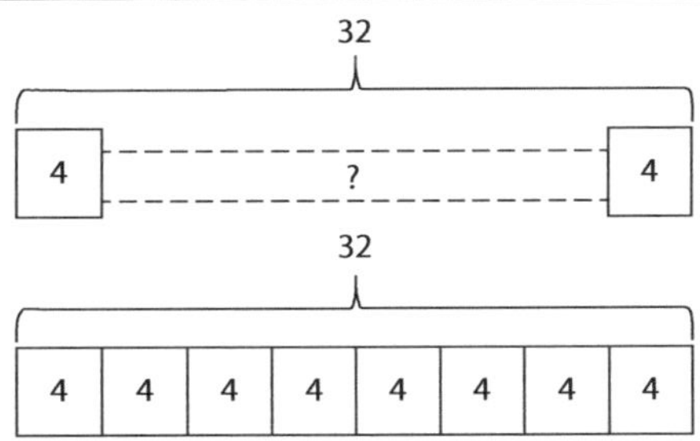 **Figure 8.14** Bar models for $32 \div 4 = ?$	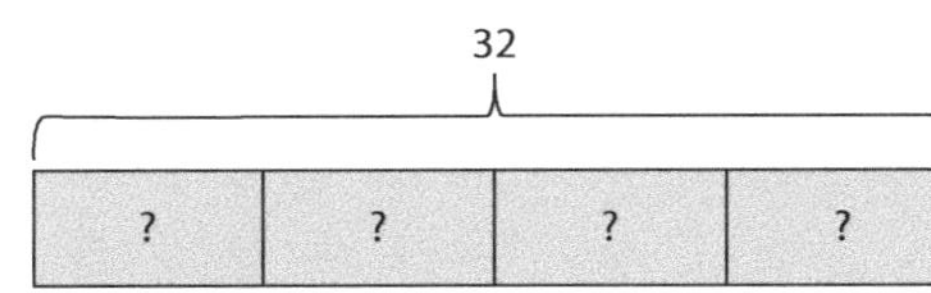 **Figure 8.15** Bar model for $32 \div 4 = ?$

A whole-school progression map outlining which models and representations should be used and when can provide a structured approach. This ensures that all teachers use a coherent set of models and representations that build progressively from EYFS to Year 6 and are introduced at an appropriate stage. This structured approach prevents pupils from relying too heavily on certain representations while missing others that could enhance their conceptual understanding. Pupils develop a deeper understanding of maths when they use multiple representations to explore concepts (Nunes et al., 2009). However, it's not enough for different teachers to use different representations in isolation. Teachers must explicitly show and explain the connections between them, highlighting how, for example, a number line, a bar model and an array can all represent subtraction or multiplication. Without these links being made clear, pupils may see the models as disconnected strategies rather than as part of a unified understanding of maths. When models are used progressively and consistently, and their relationship is made explicit, pupils can make connections between different areas of maths, strengthening their overall fluency and reasoning skills. To do this, follow these steps:

1. Audit current practice – Gather samples of planning and books from across the school and note which models, manipulatives and representations are used. Identify any inconsistencies or gaps across the school.
2. Identify key concepts – Choose one area of maths to begin with, for example place value or multiplication. List all the National Curriculum in England objectives for that concept and break it down into strands where appropriate.
3. Select core representations – Choose a small selection of core models, manipulatives and representations that best support conceptual understanding for each concept.
4. Sequence representations – Link your chosen representations to the strands and put them in order of when they will be introduced based on what is appropriate for each year group.
5. Make the links explicit – Include notes or plan professional development sessions on how teachers can connect the representations and emphasise that different representations shouldn't be taught in isolation, but used to deepen understanding and encourage flexible thinking.
6. Model and embed – Work alongside teachers to use the new progression materials when planning maths and then give them time to embed this into their practice.

7 Evaluate and adapt – Look for evidence of consistent use of models, manipulatives and representations during book looks and learning walks, and use pupil voice to understand how pupils are using and connecting representations. Make tweaks and edits along the way where necessary.

A structured progression map can support teacher confidence and ongoing PD. When teachers are clear about which models to use and how they should be introduced, they can spend more time focusing on effective pedagogy rather than deciding which representation to choose. A clear framework also promotes collaborative planning and PD, where staff can share best practices in using models effectively; observe how representations are introduced in different year groups; and ensure alignment in the teaching of key concepts across classes.

In practice: a models, manipulatives and representations progression map for recognising and identifying fractions

YEAR GROUP:	MODEL/MANIPULATIVE/ REPRESENTATION	CONCEPT
EYFS	**Real life objects like fruit and toys**	**Sharing and fair distribution**
1	A piece of paper folded in halves and quarters Rectangles and circles split into halves and quarters	Recognising equal parts Recognising and naming halves and quarters
2	Rectangles and circles split into halves, quarters and thirds Numicon with one peg in one hole	Recognising halves, quarters and thirds Writing unit fractions
3	Bar model split into fractions with a denominator up to 12 Number line split into fractions with a denominator up to 12	Recognising unit and non-unit fractions Recognising and using fractions as numbers
4	Bar model Area model Fraction wall	Recognising families of common equivalent fractions

YEAR GROUP:	MODEL/MANIPULATIVE/ REPRESENTATION	CONCEPT
EYFS	**Real life objects like fruit and toys**	**Sharing and fair distribution**
5	Fraction wall Cuisenaire rods	Identify and name equivalent fractions of a given fraction
6	Cuisenaire rods Number line	Use common multiples to express fractions in the same denomination

Systematic introduction of manipulatives

A common debate among maths leaders and teachers is whether pupils should be free to choose their own manipulatives to support their mathematical thinking. Sometimes, independent selection of resources can be a valuable skill. For example, in a Year 4 classroom where pupils have had explicit instruction on using bar models, number lines and place value counters for different types of problems, the teacher might set a multi-step word problem involving money and change. At this stage of learning, pupils are familiar with a range of representations and have practised applying them in varied contexts. They aren't guessing or grabbing manipulatives at random – they're drawing on a bank of taught strategies and representations to make informed decisions. This supports metacognitive development and shows that independence can be powerful after secure foundations have been laid. Expecting pupils to self-select manipulatives before they have been explicitly taught how and why to use them can lead to confusion, inefficiency and a lack of deep understanding. Where pupils choose their own resources, they are less likely to see the maths (NCETM, 2020).

Research by Fuson & Briars (1990) highlights that manipulatives are most effective when they are introduced systematically with clear teacher guidance. Pupils do not automatically know how to use resources like Cuisenaire rods, place value counters or bar models to support their learning. They do, however, quickly work out how to use them to build towers and other objects, often while the teacher is talking! Without structured teaching, pupils may use them in superficial or ineffective ways, leading to misconceptions rather than clarity.

Monitoring and evaluating the impact of models, manipulatives and structures

To ensure that models and representations are used effectively, you will need to monitor classroom practice and provide feedback. This can be done through learning walks, book looks and pupil voice. You want to know whether teachers are using models and representations meaningfully and appropriately and if pupils are engaging with them. You also want to see evidence of the pupils utilising the models and representations that they have been taught either when making jottings or drawing out problems. You will gain valuable insights from discussing maths with pupils to see if they find using manipulatives and pictorial representations helpful and if they can discuss how they use them in lessons.

It is important to evaluate not just whether models and representations are being used or what models and representations are being used, but how well they are supporting learning. If pupils are using manipulatives without making connections or are unable to transition to abstract reasoning, this indicates a need for further PD.

Questions for reflection

- Do teachers feel confident in selecting and using models and representations effectively?
- Are pupils able to move between concrete, pictorial and abstract representations flexibly and confidently?
- How can we provide PD that helps staff understand when and why to use specific models, representations and structures?
- How do we currently assess the effectiveness of models, representations and structures in our school?

Example PD session: using models in mathematical learning

Here is an example of what a PD session on using mathematical models could look like.

TIMING SUGGESTION	SESSION GUIDANCE
5 mins	• Discuss the purpose of using concrete, pictorial and abstract representations to bridge the gap between abstract concepts and tangible understanding. • Mention the role of models in reducing cognitive load and supporting deeper understanding (Sweller, 1988).

5 mins	• Explain/remind staff about the CPA model of introducing and teaching concepts in primary maths:
	  • Concrete: Explain the importance of physical manipulatives (e.g. counters, Dienes and Cuisenaire rods) in helping pupils understand basic mathematical concepts.
	  • Pictorial: Discuss how visual representations (e.g. number lines, bar models and arrays) link the concrete stage to abstract notation, reinforcing conceptual understanding.
	  • Abstract: Show how pupils progress to using symbols and formal notation. Emphasise that the abstract stage doesn't always need to come last but should be used alongside the concrete and pictorial stages.

10 mins	• Explain that while CPA is a helpful framework, it's essential not to follow it rigidly in every case. Teachers should select representations based on the concept being taught and the learning needs of their pupils. • Introduce Cuisenaire rods and explain that they can support conceptual understanding across year groups. • Briefly explain what Cuisenaire rods are (coloured rods of different lengths that represent different values) and highlight that their power lies in their flexibility and in representing structure, not just quantity. • State that the goal is to build confidence in when and how to use them effectively. • Give staff time to explore using the Cuisenaire rods by asking them to make trains or pictures using the rods.
5 mins	• Ask: Have you used Cuisenaire rods in your teaching? If so, when and for what? • Gather quick examples on a flipchart. Highlight variation and gaps. • Clarify that this session is about exploring their consistent, progressive use across the whole school.

TIMING SUGGESTION	SESSION GUIDANCE

20 mins	• Model key examples of how rods can be used across phases:
	  • EYFS/KS1: Number composition, subitising, pattern making, early addition and subtraction (e.g. orange rod and red rod together match a dark green rod).
	  • LKS2: Multiplicative reasoning, number facts, commutativity (e.g. 3 rods of 4 equal 2 rods of 6), understanding times tables, early fraction equivalence.
	  • UKS2: Fractions, scaling, ratio, algebraic thinking (e.g. representing 1:2 or exploring equations like $x + 2 = 5$).
	• Use a visualiser or video to model this practically.
	• Ask staff to try a short task with rods and share what mathematical ideas they can represent.

10 mins	• Emphasise that Cuisenaire rods are not just about visualising number—they are about seeing structure. • Link to arithmetic structures: part-whole relationships, comparison, equivalence. • Discuss how rods can support progression to bar models and formal written methods. • Explore a misconception (e.g. treating rods like counters) and discuss how to address it.
5 mins	• Recap: how rods reveal structure, develop fluency and foster reasoning. • Highlight importance of teacher confidence and clarity in using them purposefully, not performatively. • Action step: Ask each teacher to use the rods in the next fortnight and to bring back a pupil work sample or photo to the next meeting for shared reflection.

Explore further

- *Visible Maths* (2019) by Peter Mattock
- *Mathematics Explained for Primary Teachers* (2024) by Derek Haylock
- *American Educator's* article 'Ask the Cognitive Scientist: Do Manipulatives Help Students Learn?' (2017) by Daniel Willingham

Chapter summary

- Models, manipulatives and structures support conceptual understanding and reduce cognitive load; subject leaders should promote purposeful and consistent use across year groups.

- The CPA model enables pupils to build deep understanding by using physical manipulations, visual representations and abstract calculation, which should be used flexibly, not rigidly.
- Using representations like bar models to expose structures, for example comparison, augmentation and partitive division helps pupils understand what operations actually mean.
- Inconsistent models, language and representations across classes can lead to misconceptions and cognitive overload, so you could use a progression map with explicit links between representations.
- Pupils should not be expected to self-select manipulatives before being explicitly taught how and when to use them.

9 Variation

Variation theory is a powerful but often misunderstood or underused aspect of maths teaching that helps pupils make connections between mathematical ideas, deepen their understanding and develop fluency. This chapter explores how variation can be used effectively in primary maths lessons, supporting both conceptual understanding and procedural fluency. As a maths leader, your role is to ensure that variation is embedded meaningfully in teaching, enabling pupils to see patterns, generalise and apply their knowledge flexibly. Teachers should be ready to look for opportunities for variation when planning maths learning.

What is variation theory?

Variation theory is based on the principle that learning happens when pupils focus on what changes and what stays the same (Marton & Booth, 1997). It is underpinned by research into how humans perceive patterns and learn from contrasts. According to Marton (2014), effective learning occurs when pupils experience structured variation, allowing them to notice key features of a concept and make sense of its underlying structure.

The NCETM (2024) emphasises the role of variation in developing deep understanding, highlighting that effective teaching should carefully sequence examples to expose mathematical relationships. Variation is essential for developing problem solving as it encourages pupils to generalise mathematical patterns and apply their learning flexibly.

Types of variation

Gu et al. (2017) identified two main types of variation: conceptual and procedural. Conceptual variation involves showing different representations, examples and non-examples of the same concept to deepen understanding. The goal is to help pupils see what the concept is by varying how it is presented, while keeping the concept constant. Procedural variation involves designing a sequence of questions or problems that vary methodically to highlight patterns in procedures or steps. The goal is to develop fluency and flexibility by varying aspects of the method or the numbers involved, while keeping the overall structure of the procedure consistent.

Structured variation provides multiple entry points into learning, ensuring that pupils develop a conceptual understanding that is not reliant on memorised rules. Using variation can make mathematical ideas more accessible and meaningful. While explicit teaching is still the most effective and efficient route to pupils learning, variation instils good habits for young mathematicians of being curious and looking for patterns or changes along the way.

Conceptual variation

Conceptual variation is designed to help pupils identify the essential features of a mathematical concept by experiencing it in different forms. It challenges pupils to explore what a concept is and isn't, by varying the way it is presented while keeping the underlying structure constant. For example, when teaching the concept of a square, a teacher might show squares of different sizes, orientations and colours, alongside non-examples such as rectangles or rhombuses. Pupils would be asked to identify which shapes are squares and justify their reasoning. This helps them focus on the defining properties of a square (four equal sides and four right angles), rather than irrelevant features like size or position.

Research suggests that exposing pupils to multiple representations of a concept enhances their ability to apply knowledge flexibly (Watson & Mason, 2006). Marton & Booth (1997) explain that learning occurs when pupils can distinguish what is fundamental to a concept and what can be altered. In primary maths, conceptual variation can be used to strengthen understanding in areas such as number sense, place value, fractions and properties of shapes.

In practice: examples of conceptual variation

The number five:

- five counters on a ten-frame
- the numeral 5
- a tally
- a die face showing five dots
- a set of five pencils
- a Numicon five.

Multiplication as repeated equal groups:

- three groups of four counters
- an array showing three rows of four
- repeated addition $4 + 4 + 4$
- a bar model showing three parts of four
- a number line with a jump of four, three times.

One half:

- a circle split into two equal parts
- a bar split in two with one side shaded
- a ten frame with five counters
- sharing six cubes between two people
- the written fraction $\frac{1}{2}$.

When pupils are exposed to only one way of seeing a concept, they may overgeneralise rules or develop rigid thinking. For example, if pupils only ever see one quarter as one quarter of a circle, they might struggle to recognise a quarter of other shapes or a set of objects.

By using standard examples, non-standard examples and non-examples, pupils can begin to generalise and confirm what something is and what it isn't. Standard examples are ones that we see in everyday representations or typical representations that spring to mind, whereas non-standard examples are those that are still correct but sometimes not immediately recognisable. Non-examples are those that could trick pupils and do not have the underlying structure or features of the concept. Table 4 below shows examples of each.

Procedural variation

Procedural variation is a powerful teaching tool that focuses on varying the methods used to solve mathematical problems while keeping the underlying concept the same. Unlike conceptual variation, which helps pupils understand what a mathematical concept is, procedural variation helps pupils to see connections between different procedures. There are three forms of procedural variation:

Table 4 Types of variation

PHASE	CONTENT	VARIATION IN EXAMPLES		
		STANDARD EXAMPLES	NON-STANDARD EXAMPLES	NON-EXAMPLES
EYFS	What makes eight?	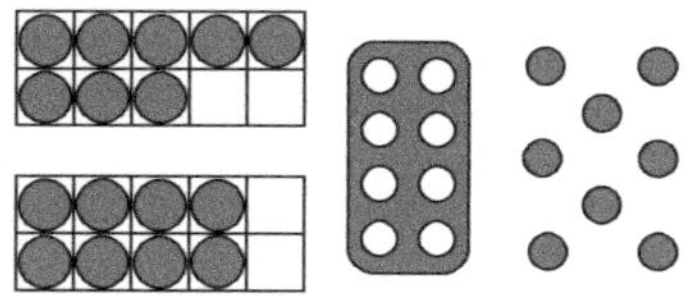 **Figure 9.1** Sets of eight counters shown in ten-frames, Numicon and like a playing card	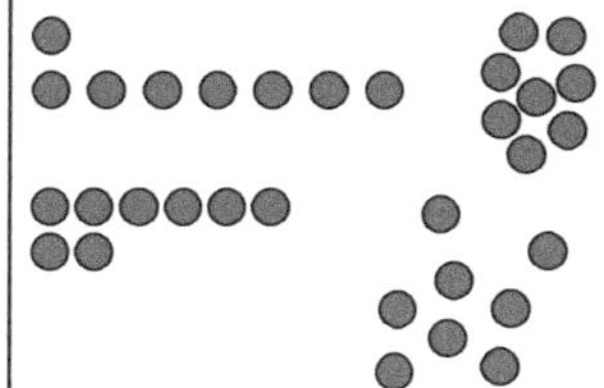 **Figure 9.2** Sets of eight counters shown in random positions	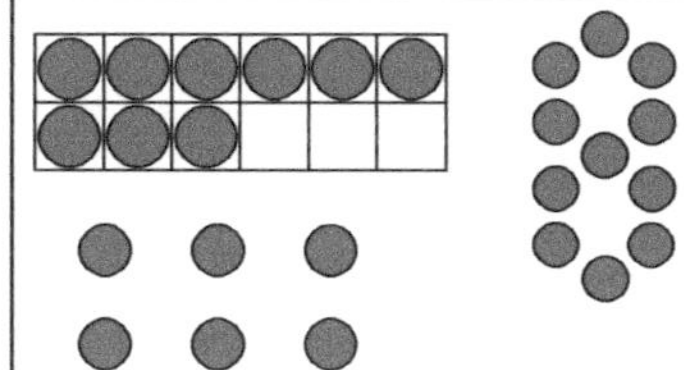 **Figure 9.3** Sets of nine, six and 11 counters that could be mistaken for eight
KS1	What makes a triangle?	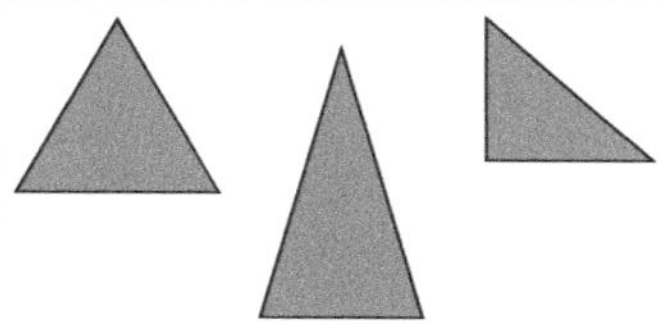 **Figure 9.4** Equilateral, isosceles and right-angled triangles	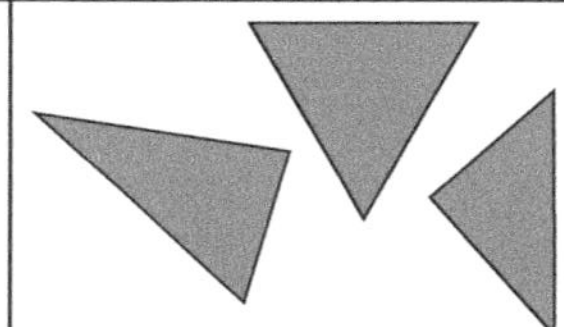 **Figure 9.5** Triangles in 'unusual' orientations	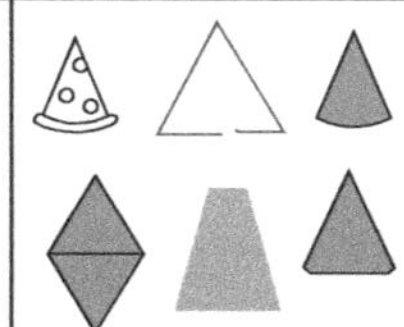 **Figure 9.6** Non-triangular shapes that could be mistaken for triangles
KS2	What makes $\frac{1}{10}$?	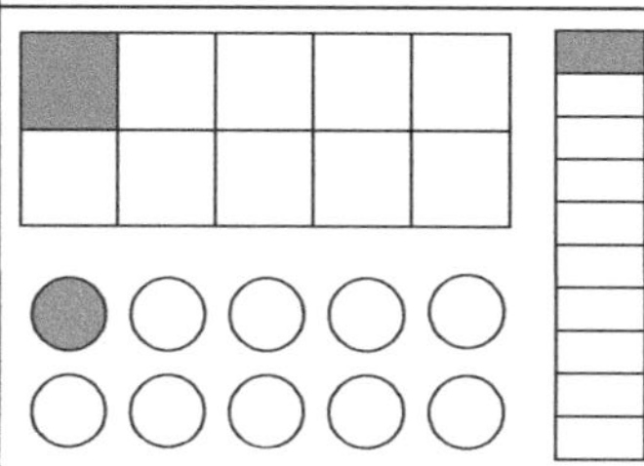 **Figure 9.7** One tenth shown in a 5×2 grid, 1×10 bar and array of ten counters	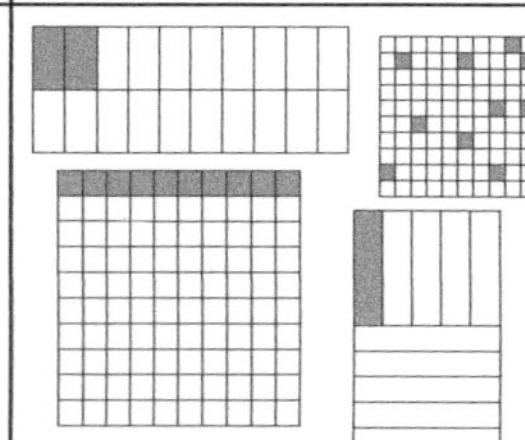 **Figure 9.8** One tenth shown in a 10×2 grid, 100-square and an oblong with vertical and horizontal equal parts	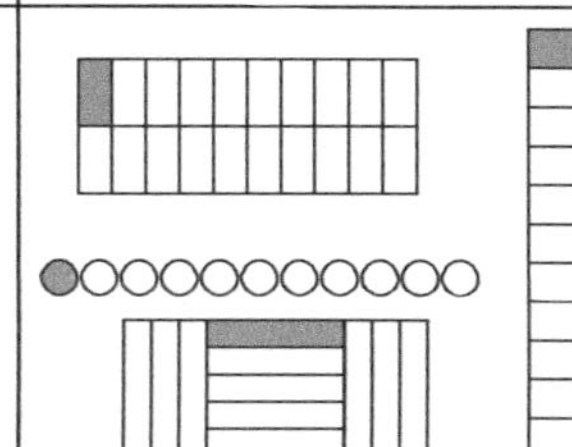 **Figure 9.9** Diagrams showing potential misconceptions of what one tenth looks like

- varying a problem to vary the conditions, change the results and prompt generalisations to reinforce a concept
- using multiple methods to solve a problem to foster problem-solving strategies
- using multiple applications of a method to expose the underlying concept (Lai & Murray, 2012).

PHASE	CONTENT	VARIETY No rhyme or reason to the order of the questions	PROCEDURAL VARIATION Varying one part of a problem at a time in a sequence of questions to expose patterns and relationships in the numbers
KS1	Adding two-digit numbers	45 + 15 29 + 20 67 + 22 56 + 24 29 + 87	36 + 21 36 + 22 36 + 32 46 + 32 56 + 33
KS2	Multiplying decimals and integers	2.5 x 4 0.7 x 6 5.5 x 8 9.3 x 7 3.2 x 3	3.1 x 4 3.2 x 4 3.3 x 4 3.5 x 4 3.5 x 8

Where certain parts of a problem remain constant, and tweaks are made to one part of each problem in a sequence, pupils can be encouraged to notice first and solve second.

In practice: guiding pupils through questions

The teacher might say, 'Before we start calculating, I want you to look carefully at the numbers. Don't work out any answers just yet. What do you notice about the first four questions?'

The teacher waits for the pupils to respond. Example responses might be: 'They're all multiplied by 4.' or 'The first number goes up by 0.1 each time.'

The teacher might reply, 'We're increasing the multiplicand by a tenth each time, but keeping the multiplier the same. What do you think will happen to the answers?'

The teacher waits for the pupils to predict what will happen to the answers. A prediction could be, 'The answers will go up by 0.4 each time.'

So the teacher would say, 'Great prediction! Let's test it out by working them out one at a time.'

They would work through the answers together before the teacher asks, 'Now, look at the last one: 3.5×8. What's changed?'

The pupils might say, 'The 3.5 stayed the same, but now we're multiplying by 8 instead of 4.'

'So now we're asking a different question. What impact does doubling the multiplier have on the product?'

Research by Rohrer & Taylor (2007) suggests that varying practice is more effective for long-term retention than repetitive drills. If pupils are exposed to variation in practice tasks, they are more likely to understand the relationships between numbers rather than simply recalling isolated facts.

Supporting pupils with SEND

For some pupils with SEND, variation can be particularly beneficial as it allows them to see the same concept in different ways and at their own pace. Teaching all pupils with variation in mind allows for gradual learning with appropriate scaffolding. Teachers can introduce simpler variations first, before gradually increasing complexity. Using visual representations alongside number sentences ensures that pupils can see the relationships between numbers, helping them to make connections more easily.

The role of the subject leader in embedding variation

As a maths leader, one of your key responsibilities is ensuring that variation is embedded across the school. Many teachers may naturally incorporate some variation into their teaching but may not be aware of its full potential or how to structure it effectively. Supporting teachers to move beyond random variety towards conceptual and procedural variation is essential for deepening pupils' understanding.

One way to achieve this is through PD. Providing PD on variation theory, with practical examples of conceptual and procedural variation, can help teachers design lessons that build understanding more effectively. Encouraging collaborative lesson planning can also ensure that structured variation is embedded consistently across different year groups.

Regular lesson observations and pupil discussions can provide valuable insights into how well variation is being used in classrooms. Key questions for you to consider when evaluating the impact of variation in teaching may include the following:

- Are pupils exposed to different representations of mathematical concepts?
- Are they encouraged to explore different strategies for solving problems?
- Are they making connections between different areas of maths?

Questions for reflection

- How is variation currently used in our school's maths teaching? Is it deliberate, or is it more incidental?
- Do teachers in our school understand the difference between variety and variation?
- Do our fluency and practice tasks incorporate structured variation, or do they rely on repetitive drills?
- How do we ensure that variation starts in EYFS?

Example PD session: developing experiences of variation

Here is an example of what a PD session on variation could look like.

TIMING SUGGESTION	SESSION GUIDANCE
15 mins	• Begin by asking teachers to reflect on their own maths experiences: Did they learn by memorising methods or by exploring patterns and relationships? • Introduce the key principles of variation theory, using research from Gu et al. (2004) and Marton (2014). • Clarify the difference between variety and variation.
10 mins	• Split teachers into phase teams. • Provide curriculum materials and past lesson tasks and ask them to identify where variation is used well and where it could be improved. • Ask each group to write examples of strong variation practice and missed opportunities on sticky notes.

10 mins	• Provide an example topic, e.g. addition. Start with something that everyone will confidently be able to write questions on.
	• Compare two different sets:
	  • random variety (e.g. different multiplication facts)
	  • structured variation (e.g. systematically changing one element at a time).
	• Discuss which set will help pupils develop connections more effectively.
	• Ask teachers to create a set of variation-based questions for that concept.

5 mins	• Discuss whether pupils are experiencing variation consistently. • Share ideas on how to introduce variation earlier and build on it progressively.
15 mins	• Ask teams to look at what is coming up in their maths lessons. • Give them time to look at the suggested planning materials and tasks and to enhance them using variation. • Explain that, by the end of the 15 minutes, they should have written something that can be used in an upcoming lesson.
5 mins	• Each group shares one key change they will make to their teaching. • Discuss how you can evaluate the impact of variation in lessons.

Explore further

- Third Space Learning's blog *What Is Variation Theory? A Guide For Primary Maths Teachers* (2025a) by Neil Almond: https://thirdspacelearning.com/blog/variation-theory/
- *Reflect, Expect, Check, Explain: Sequences and Behaviour to Enable Mathematical Thinking in the Classroom* (2020) by Craig Barton
- *Mathematical Tasks: the Bridge between Teaching and Learning* (2020) by Chris McGrane and Mark McCourt

Chapter summary

- Variation theory is about structuring examples to highlight patterns, relationships and underlying mathematical structures.
- Conceptual variation helps pupils identify key properties of mathematical ideas by exploring multiple representations.
- Procedural variation exposes connections between strategies and problems.
- Intelligent practice uses systematic variation to ensure that fluency practice strengthens conceptual understanding rather than becoming rote repetition.
- All pupils benefit from structured variation because it provides a carefully considered route to making connections and understanding concepts.

10 Vocabulary and stem sentences

Vocabulary is key to unlocking mathematical understanding and thinking. When pupils can use mathematical vocabulary fluently and confidently, they are able to make sense of concepts, articulate their reasoning and engage in problem solving.

According to The Oxford Language Report (2023-2024), there has been an increase in the number of pupils falling behind with vocabulary acquisition in schools across the United Kingdom. This won't be a surprise to many of you, but it is crucial for us to remind ourselves that we are facing an uphill climb when teaching any subject, especially one as complex as maths. In its 2022 research review of English, Ofsted acknowledged the link between vocabulary development and academic achievement and made it clear that vocabulary teaching should be at the forefront of teachers' and leaders' minds.

This chapter will explore the importance of explicit teaching of vocabulary in primary maths and how to optimise the use of stem sentences in improving mathematical understanding and explanations.

Types of vocabulary

Beck and McKeown (1985) suggest that we can look at vocabulary in three tiers.

- **Tier 1 words** are those that we come across in everyday life and are commonly used in spoken language as well as in writing. These words don't generally require high levels of instruction and are often acquired through exposure. Pupils with speech and language disorders will sometimes need Tier 1 words explicitly taught as they are less likely to pick up words merely through exposure.
- **Tier 2 words** are sophisticated or academic words found across a range of subjects that are essential to understanding complex concepts. They include terms such as 'compare', 'evaluate', 'examine', 'problem' and 'solve'.

- **Tier 3 words** are content-specific words that are related to a particular subject area or domain. They include terms such as 'addend', 'minuend', 'quotient' and 'subtrahend'.

By categorising vocabulary into Tier 1, Tier 2, and Tier 3 words, we can strategically target our instruction to scaffold our pupils' language development and deepen their comprehension of mathematical concepts.

Take a look at the example Tier 2 and Tier 3 words above. As you can see, the Tier 2 words will not only come up in maths lessons. These words will come up again and again in different contexts, and will require explicit teaching so that all pupils can understand their meaning. The Tier 3 words will also require explicit teaching, but these are words that will likely come up only in the context of the lesson that is being taught. These words should be taught within maths lessons, whereas the Tier 2 words should be included in general vocabulary-teaching sessions.

Vocabulary progression and shared definitions

Acknowledging the differences between Tier 1, Tier 2 and Tier 3 words will support teachers to know how and when to teach them. As a subject leader, you will want to have an oversight of which words will come up, when they come up, how frequently they come up and how they are being taught. This is where a vocabulary progression document with agreed definitions can be utilised. Pupils in your school will come across over 100 new words in their maths lessons. Many of these words (e.g. 'triangle', 'subtract' and 'fraction') will come up again and again. If every teacher in your school is using a slightly different definition for each word, this will become confusing for the pupils and make it much harder to learn the meaning and apply it.

Ideally, shared definitions will be accurate, concise and accessible so that the pupils have the best chance of learning the plethora of vocabulary that they will encounter in maths and every other subject.

Creating a vocabulary progression document

You want your subject to be successful and you want to drive improvement, so you may decide to create a shared vocabulary progression document during subject leadership time that you have coming up. This is one way to introduce a vocabulary progression, but it might not be the most effective or get the most buy-in from staff.

The quickest thing for you as a subject leader is to do all the deep thinking yourself or use something that another school has done and then present it to your colleagues as a finished document. However, the best learning for our teachers can come from opportunities where they have been part of the process and given the time and space to think deeply too.

Kieran Mackle (2020, p.193) says, 'For me, the time we spend planning, preferably with colleagues, is time that should be dedicated, in some part, to identifying the language we will deliberately use during the coming sequence of lessons', and that the power of this time with colleagues should not be underestimated. This could be done during planning time either in teams or when you are working alongside teachers, or it could be done during ring-fenced PD time (as suggested in the professional development section at the end of this chapter).

Case study: shared definitions

Naima is maths leader at a diverse, inner-city primary school. During lesson drop-ins, she notices inconsistencies in how key mathematical terms are being used across different year groups. Words such as 'value', 'digit' and 'number' are being interpreted in various ways by pupils, leading to confusion, misconceptions and inaccurate written answers.

Naima recognises that a shared, consistent language is essential for building mathematical understanding across the school. She sets out to lead a whole-staff initiative to agree on clear, age-appropriate definitions for the most frequently used mathematical terms in the curriculum. Her aim is to ensure that all pupils, regardless of class or year group, hear and use these terms consistently.

Step 1: Staff survey and 'listening walks'

Naima begins by carrying out a brief, anonymous online staff survey, asking teachers to list the mathematical vocabulary they find themselves explaining repeatedly. While the whole school are working on place value at the start of the year, Naima also conducts listening walks across the school, noting the language used by teachers and pupils during maths lessons. This helps her to identify common terms that are either misunderstood or explained in different ways.

Step 2: PD

Next, Naima leads a staff meeting focused on mathematical language. Teachers are grouped in cross-phase teams and asked to define key words in simple terms. These definitions are then shared and refined through professional dialogue. Naima facilitates the discussion to ensure that the definitions are not only accurate but also accessible to pupils from Key Stage 1 through to Upper Key Stage 2. She uses the Mathematics Glossary for KS1-KS3 from the NCETM (2014a) to support teachers' discussions, but she encourages them to refine their own shared definitions.

Step 3: Finalising and embedding the vocabulary

Once the definitions are agreed, Naima compiles them into a school-wide glossary and creates accompanying posters for classrooms. She also encourages staff to refer to the definitions explicitly during teaching and to model their use in full sentences. Over time, these definitions become part of the school's mathematical culture, supporting consistency in planning, teaching and assessment.

Some of the agreed definitions:

Numeral – A symbol used to write numbers.
Digit – The numerals 0, 1, 2, 3, 4, 5, 6, 7, 8 and 9, which form part of a number.
Number – One or more digits that represent a quantity or value.
Value – How much a digit is worth, depending on its place in the number.
Sum – The result of adding two or more numbers.
Naima's initiative leads to improved pupil explanations and more consistent teaching. Next, she plans to create a glossary to share with parents and carers.

Explicit teaching

Quigley (2018) lays out three pillars for vocabulary teaching: explicit teaching, incidental teaching and cultivating word consciousness. Incidental vocabulary teaching is most often required when reading books or texts where words come up that we haven't planned for. Pupils might ask what a word means and you'll briefly explore it before putting it back into the context of what was being read. While this may come up in maths sometimes, when reading questions or problems, we spend far more time explicitly teaching vocabulary so that we can unlock pupils' understanding right there in the moment.

Explicit teaching requires careful planning to teach the meaning of specific words or terms intentionally and systematically, through modelling and practice. By explicitly teaching new language in maths lessons, we can equip our pupils with what they need to access questions and engage in mathematical thinking and reasoning.

Guiding principles

The following are some guiding principles for explicit teaching in maths.

1. Give pupils ample time to say the word out loud.
2. Provide examples and non-examples to zoom in to a definition.
3. Provide opportunities to use the word.
4. Engage in regular word retrieval.

Let's explore each of these in more depth.

1. Give pupils ample time to say the word out loud.

While it might seem obvious, we cannot underestimate the benefit of practising saying a word out loud and exploring it verbally before attempting to define or use it. Pupils can practise the word aloud in different voices, volumes and speeds; this could be independently, in pairs and chorally as a class. You might clap out the syllables or segment it into its component phonemes, too. All of this will instil these behaviours in the pupils for when they learn new words independently.

2. Provide examples and non-examples to zoom into a definition.

Using examples and non-examples is a powerful instructional strategy that isn't limited to vocabulary teaching. However, it is particularly helpful when teaching new words, as it provides pupils with a clear understanding of what a word is and what it isn't. By presenting examples, the pupils can grasp the essential characteristics of the new word. By presenting non-examples, we can reinforce the underlying concept of the word as well as dispel misconceptions. Once the pupils have explored concrete examples and ruled out non-examples, they can begin to define a word. While it is a worthwhile endeavour to get them to

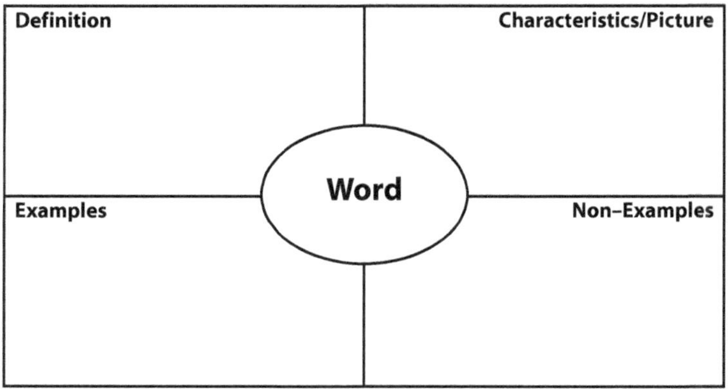

Figure 10.1 Blank Frayer model with explanation of what goes in each box

collaborate to create a definition, as a subject leader you will want to ensure that teachers have clear definitions to guide the pupils towards.

You might want to introduce a graphic organiser like the Frayer Model (see Figure 10.1), which provides a structure for the explicit instruction of new language.

A Frayer Model is a simple way of representing the learning process for a new word that can be used when exploring examples and non-examples, and then when defining the word. Promoting this sort of curiosity around words will continue to instil good habits around vocabulary learning.

In Figure 10.2, you can see how the word 'triangle', which could be seen as an 'everyday' (Tier 1) maths word, is broken down to clarify the meaning. The non-examples highlight misconceptions to solidify the true definition of what a triangle is.

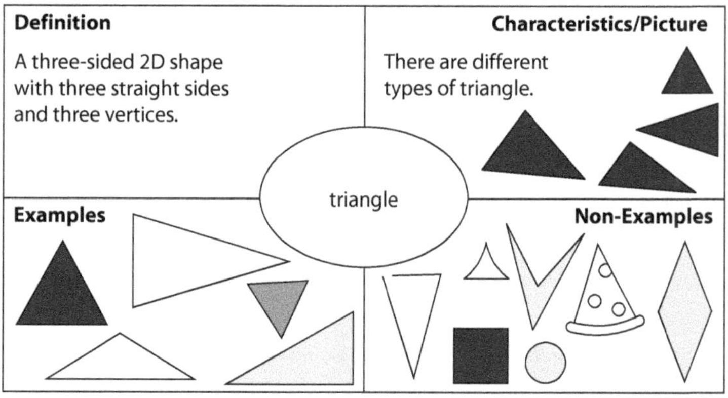

Figure 10.2 Completed Frayer model for the word 'triangle'

3. Provide opportunities to use the word.

When teaching Tier 3 words, for example 'numerator', pupils will encounter the word in or before a lesson involving fractions. They should then have opportunities to use and apply the word in structured tasks set by the teacher, such as during 'think, pair, share' activities or answering questions verbally or in writing. The word will come up because it is crucial for their understanding in that lesson.

When you are teaching Tier 2 words in more general vocabulary lessons, the pupils should be given a chance to use the word. They might be given something to read and answer some simple questions on; there might be a cloze procedure task; they might have to use it in a sentence. Whatever it is, they should be given the opportunity to use the word during instruction as well as later on in other lessons.

4. Engage in regular word retrieval.

For pupils to become fluent and confident with using new vocabulary, they need to engage in retrieval tasks to ensure the word goes into their long-term memory. Word retrieval might involve a low-stakes quiz, multiple-choice questions, informal quizzing in class using a knowledge organiser or even a retrieval pot of words that gets used when there's a spare five minutes during the day. For pupils to use the word in their verbal and written explanations, they need to remember it and be secure in what it means.

Etymology and morphology

Etymology is the study of the origin of words and the way words have changed over time. Utilising etymology to teach mathematical vocabulary can enrich pupils' understanding of the language by enabling them to make sense of new words and encouraging curiosity around words. The English language is a complex beast, but we can begin to demystify that by exposing the pupils to the range of origins and backgrounds to the words that they are learning.

Morphology is the study of the parts of words. When we teach phonics, we think of phonemes (the smallest units of sound) and graphemes (how we represent phonemes in writing). Morphemes are the smallest units of meaning. By understanding root words and how prefixes and suffixes change them, the pupils will be able to apply this knowledge to new words.

We can use morphology and etymology to explore and teach certain mathematical vocabulary. They needn't be used for every single word in the curriculum, but there will be some cases where they support understanding by making abstract words concrete.

The job of a subject leader is to expose staff to the importance of etymology and morphology and work together to decide which words should have the etymology or morphology highlighted as part of the instruction process. This can be included in the vocabulary progression document or curriculum materials so that all staff have access to it.

Table 5 below shows some examples of words that can be unpacked using etymology and morphology.

Table 5 Etymology and morphology of common maths words

WORD	ORIGIN	ROOTS	MEANING	SUPPORTING EXAMPLES
isosceles	Greek	isos – equal skelos – legs	An isosceles triangle is one with two equal sides.	 **Figure 10.3** Stick figure with isosceles triangle formed by equal legs
numerator	Latin	numerare – to number; to count	The numerator is the part that we count.	$\frac{3}{10}$ **three** tenths 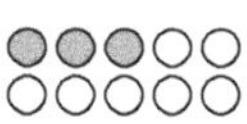 **Figure 10.4** Three counters out of ten outlined to show the numerator
denominator	Latin	denominare – to name	The denominator names the fraction.	$\frac{3}{10}$ **three** tenths 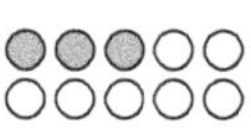 **Figure 10.5** Ten counters outlined to show the denominator

Stem sentences

In primary maths, stem sentences serve as a scaffold for unlocking understanding and structuring mathematical explanations. Stem sentences can support pupils in articulating their reasoning by offering a framework to build on. By providing pupils with stem sentences, teachers can empower them to engage in mathematical thinking.

Stem sentences can be used to make generalisations about mathematical concepts, provide a structure for giving an explanation, or express a concept using accurate vocabulary and a high standard of English. They can support pupils in approaching multi-step problems by breaking down each problem and scaffolding each step.

Table 6 below shows some examples of stem sentences that could be used in maths, in each phase of primary school.

Table 6 Example stem sentences

PHASE	CONTENT	STEM SENTENCE	EXAMPLE
EYFS	Comparing objects around the classroom	The ________ is taller than the ________.	The table is taller than the book.
KS1	Partitioning two-digit numbers	One part is ________. The other part is ________. The whole is ________.	One part is 30. The other part is 5. The whole is 35.
KS2	Exploring additive structures	If I add ____ to an addend, the sum also increases by ____.	If I add 1 to an addend, the sum also increases by 1. **39 + 20 = 59** +1 +1 **40 + 20 = 60**

These stem sentences can be used in various ways. They could be shared at the start of instruction so that the pupils have plenty of time to see them being used by their teacher to explain the concept again and again, even if the words or numbers in the gaps change. Stem sentences can be displayed on working walls, which serve as great talking points for conducting pupil voice in maths lessons as a subject leader.

A popular and effective way of using stem sentences is to fade out some of the details and words gradually. Like any good scaffold, it is removed over time so that the pupils become more independent.

Below is an example of how a stem sentence can be faded out over the course of a lesson.

1. When both factors have the same value, the product is called a square number.
2. When both ______ have the same value, the product is called a square number.
3. When both ______ have the same value, the ______ is called a square number.
4. When both ______ have the same ______, the ______ is called a square number.
5. When both ______ have the same ______, the ______ is called a ______ number.

The stem sentence could appear on a teaching slide or written on a whiteboard, and with each modelled example the teacher would remove more and more of the vocabulary. This can continue while the pupils are completing their own examples during guided practice. The stem sentence is there as an anchor point for their understanding that they can keep coming back to as they work their way through some examples, and become more confident and independent with the new subject matter. This stem sentence then becomes integral to their reasoning later on.

As with vocabulary, you could have a shared bank of stem sentences to ensure high quality stem sentences are being used and to free up teachers' minds from having to create these from scratch for every concept. You might use the same structure of PD as suggested for the vocabulary progression document and, to ensure effective implementation, you could co-plan with teachers of each year group to support them with using stem sentences effectively in their lessons.

Questions for reflection

- What is the demographic like in our school? Do our pupils come from language-rich environments?
- Are our staff aware of the vocabulary tiers and how they differ?
- How is mathematical vocabulary taught in our school? Is there a consistent approach?
- How could we generate and utilise shared definitions in our school? What would the benefits be?
- Is there a mathematical language progression in place?
- Do our pupils have access to stem sentences to structure their reasoning?

Example PD session: collaboratively creating a plan for vocabulary

Here is an example of what a PD session on planning vocabulary progression could look like.

TIMING SUGGESTION	SESSION GUIDANCE
	SESSION 1
15 mins	• Recap (or introduce if your staff haven't seen it before) the simple memory model and how pupils learn and encode information. See Chapter 2 on getting the best from the evidence. • Talk through relevant research on vocabulary teaching to set the scene for your PD.
15 mins	• Depending on the size of your school, group the teachers in phases or year group teams. • Ask them to go through the curriculum materials and pull out the language that the pupils need to understand. • Write each word on a sticky note and stick it onto a big sheet of paper for each year group.

15 mins	• Spend time looking at these words. Consider which ones come up more than once. Ask:
	  • Are there any words that surprise your staff?
	  • Do you need to introduce some words earlier or later?
	  • Do some year groups have lots more to learn than others?
	  • Do any of these words come up in other subjects?

TIMING SUGGESTION	SESSION GUIDANCE
10 mins	• Ask each group to put these words into a progression document from EYFS to Year 6. Which words should be taught, and when?
5 mins	• Ask each group to feedback and briefly discuss the advantages of each case.
After the session	• Collate the progressions into one live document online based on your expertise, the curriculum and the teachers' decisions.
SESSION 2	
Before the session	• Share the document before the next PD session so those teachers who want to can read it beforehand.
10 mins	• Give everyone time to read the vocabulary progression document. • Discuss how it relates to their current practice.
5 mins	• As a group, pick out the words that come up in multiple year groups. You might want to limit this to ten words to keep it focused, but if you have a large number of staff then consider how many words you can get through.
10 mins 10 mins	• Ask individuals to write down the definitions that they would use to teach the words. They could use their laptops or phones to check curriculum documents or online materials. • Share the definitions that everyone has come up with for each word, one at a time. How do they differ? Are any of them wrong?
25 mins	• Decide on one final shared definition for each word. • NOTE: Give this process the time that it needs. If you can't get through all of the words you've looked at, don't rush it. Come back to it in another PD session.
After the session	• Write up the agreed shared definitions in your vocabulary progression document. • Share this with all stakeholders and publish on your school website for parental reference.

Explore further

- *Closing the Vocabulary Gap* (2018) by Alex Quigley
- *Thinking Deeply about Primary Mathematics* (2020) by Kieran Mackle
- Third Space Learning's blog *How To Help Primary School Pupils Develop The Maths Language Skills They Need To Succeed In SATs* (2025) by Eliot Morgan: https://thirdspacelearning.com/blog/maths-language-skills/

Chapter summary

- Vocabulary acquisition is an uphill climb, so effective vocabulary teaching is crucial.
- Vocabulary is split into three tiers. Tier 1 words are everyday terms, Tier 2 words are academic words that span curriculum areas and Tier 3 words are content-specific words.
- Subject leaders can utilise PD time to collaborate on shared definitions and a progression for language.
- Consistent approaches can benefit teachers when planning and teaching, and pupils when learning.
- Explicit instruction, etymology and morphology and stem sentences can be used by teachers when teaching new vocabulary.

11 Assessment

Assessment is not just about generating data. When designed and used effectively, assessment can be meaningful and manageable. As a maths lead, your role is to ensure that maths assessment is used strategically across the school to support both pupil progress and teacher effectiveness. Without robust assessment protocols, we have no way of knowing if our curriculum and teaching are having the desired effect and therefore have no clear next steps. This chapter will explore the purpose of assessment, what makes effective assessment, how to use assessment data and how to make assessment meaningful.

What makes effective assessment in primary maths?

Poorly designed assessments can misrepresent pupils' understanding, create unnecessary barriers, or focus too narrowly on procedural knowledge rather than deep mathematical thinking. Effective assessments should be valid, reliable, accessible and assess both breadth and depth of mathematical understanding.

Validity

Validity refers to whether the interpretations and inferences we draw from assessment results are accurate and appropriate for their intended purpose. In maths, this means ensuring that we use assessment information to make justified conclusions about what pupils know and can do. An assessment can be highly valid for one purpose, but not necessarily for another.

For example, the Multiplication Tables Check (MTC) has strong validity for assessing rapid recall of multiplication facts. However, it would not be valid to use MTC results to make judgements about pupils' conceptual understanding of multiplication or problem-solving ability because it hasn't been designed for that.

For classroom and school-based assessments, validity often depends on alignment with the curriculum and teaching. Black and Wiliam (1998) argue that effective assessment is integrated into instruction and reflects the intended learning objectives. If assessments are disconnected from what has been taught, they can't necessarily provide meaningful evidence of pupil learning.

As a maths subject leader, it's important to regularly review assessment materials and ensure that the inferences drawn from them are appropriate. This means checking that assessments measure the intended mathematical knowledge and skills, and that any conclusions used to inform planning, intervention or reporting are based on sound evidence.

Here is a breakdown of the assessments in primary maths and how they link to validity:

Table 7 Types of primary maths assessment

ASSESSMENT TYPE	WHAT IT VALIDLY MEASURES	WHAT IT CAN'T VALIDLY MEASURE	EXAMPLE OF AN APPROPRIATE INFERENCE	NON-EXAMPLE OF AN INFERENCE
Multiplication Tables Check (MTC)	Recall and fluency of multiplication facts up to 12 × 12	Conceptual understanding of multiplication or application in problem solving	'Pupil A can recall multiplication facts quickly and accurately.'	'Pupil A deeply understands multiplication and can apply it in new contexts.'
Arithmetic paper (Paper 1 KS2 SATs)	Procedural fluency in written and mental calculations	Problem-solving skills, reasoning or conceptual understanding beyond calculation	'Pupil B can use written methods accurately for the four operations.'	'Pupil B is a confident mathematician who can reason about number.'
Reasoning paper (Papers 2 and 3 KS2 SATs)	Ability to apply known concepts to unfamiliar problems; mathematical reasoning and explanation	Speed of recall or fluency in basic facts	'Pupil C can apply strategies to solve problems.'	'Pupil C has rapid recall of number facts.'
Formative assessment, e.g. hinge question	Understanding of a specific concept or step within a lesson	Broader attainment or overall understanding	'Most pupils have grasped the concept of regrouping in subtraction.'	'The class is secure in subtraction.'

ASSESSMENT TYPE	WHAT IT VALIDLY MEASURES	WHAT IT CAN'T VALIDLY MEASURE	EXAMPLE OF AN APPROPRIATE INFERENCE	NON-EXAMPLE OF AN INFERENCE
Teacher observation of verbal pupil explanation	Reasoning processes, mathematical language and conceptual understanding in real time	Long-term retention or fluency	'Pupil D can justify why one fraction is larger than another.'	'Pupil D has embedded this concept in their long-term memory.'
Low-stakes retrieval quiz	Retention of previously taught facts and methods	Depth of understanding or reasoning ability	'Pupil E has retained key place value facts from last term.'	'Pupil E fully understands the structure of our number system.'

Reliability

Reliability refers to the consistency of an assessment, whether it produces stable and dependable results over time and across different groups of pupils under similar conditions (Harlen, 2007). In other words, a reliable maths assessment would give similar results if the same pupil took it again under comparable circumstances. Reliability is important because inconsistent assessments can make it difficult for teachers and leaders to track progress or identify genuine learning needs. High reliability gives leaders and teachers confidence that changes in pupil outcomes reflect real learning, not inconsistencies in assessment design or administration. To improve reliability, teachers and leaders should:

- use consistent test design to remove unnecessary barriers and improve familiarity
- avoid ambiguous or language-heavy questions to increase the number of pupils who understand what is being asked
- standardise the administration of tests so that the conditions remain the same or at least similar each time
- combine multiple sources of evidence, e.g. quizzes, observations and tests, to avoid over-reliance on one type of assessment
- review end of unit or end of term assessments to check for the above
- pilot new assessment materials on a small-scale before full implementation to identify potential reliability issues.

Accessibility

For assessments to be effective, they need to be accessible to all pupils, including pupils with SEND and those learning EAL. Assessment should measure mathematical understanding rather than literacy skills, processing speed or other unrelated factors. This is a difficult task, but as much as possible we shouldn't let a child's literacy attainment impact their maths attainment. Subject leaders can regularly review assessments to ensure they do not create unnecessary barriers for certain groups of pupils, and review the use of technology to enhance accessibility.

You can work with your SENDCo or EAL lead in school to identify potential barriers, for example complex sentence structures, culturally unfamiliar contexts or excessive instructions. Where appropriate, you can rewrite questions to make them more accessible to your pupils. You could trial revised questions with a small group of pupils with differing needs and use their feedback to refine your in-school assessments.

Of course, this isn't possible with national standardised assessments, so you could also work alongside your SENDCo on the sort of access arrangements that might be available for pupils at the end of KS2. Then, you could put these in place for pupils when they are completing assessments in other year groups to get a more valid result.

Breadth and depth

Traditional maths assessments often focus heavily on arithmetic, prioritising speed and accuracy over conceptual understanding and reasoning. However, effective assessment should reflect the full scope of mathematical learning, including fluency, reasoning and problem solving.

Kilpatrick et al. (2001) emphasise that a well-rounded maths education includes procedural fluency, conceptual understanding, and strategic competence. Assessments should reflect this balance rather than focusing solely on correct answers. A practical approach to assessing reasoning and problem solving is the use of open-ended tasks and low-threshold, high-ceiling problems – questions that all pupils can attempt but that also allow for deeper exploration and challenge.

While our statutory assessments do not include these sorts of problems, it is something that you as a maths leader can build into your school's curriculum. The use of these open-ended assessment tasks can give you and the teachers a good measure of your pupils' understanding and ability to apply their knowledge. These questions will take longer to mark so to avoid teachers feeling overwhelmed by this, you can recommend that they have their pupils self-mark as much as possible when completing their day-to-day maths work and only use these open-ended assessment tasks sporadically.

The purpose of assessment

Assessment serves multiple functions in primary maths. First and foremost, it measures the impact of our teaching. Assessment supports teachers' understanding of what pupils know, what they need to consolidate, and what they are ready to learn next. It allows for responsive teaching, ensuring that lessons are adapted to meet the needs of all learners. Assessment also identifies gaps in understanding. Misconceptions in maths can persist if not addressed, and regular assessment ensures these are spotted early. For example, if pupils misunderstand place value, this will impact their ability to perform calculations accurately. Identifying such gaps allows teachers to provide targeted interventions before misunderstandings become ingrained (Johnson, 2025).

From a whole-school perspective, assessment provides an overview of attainment and progress across year groups. It helps to track the effectiveness of the curriculum and informs school-wide decisions. However, for assessment to be truly effective, it should actively support learning.

Striking the right balance

One of the biggest challenges in assessment is ensuring that it is both meaningful and manageable. While it is important to gather information about pupils' progress, excessive testing isn't the right strategy.

Assessments should be designed with a clear purpose. Before conducting an assessment, ask:

- What will this tell us about pupils' understanding?
- How will this information be used to improve teaching and learning?

A balanced approach to assessment includes a mix of informal, low-stakes assessments, such as questioning, discussions and retrieval tasks, and more formal assessments, such as end-of-unit quizzes and standardised tests. When thinking about assessment in maths, consider how you can avoid a culture where assessment becomes a burdensome data-gathering exercise. Instead, focus on assessments that genuinely inform teaching and provide meaningful feedback to pupils.

Assessment *for* learning vs. assessment *of* learning

Black and Wiliam (1998) suggest we separate formative and summative assessment. It is important to distinguish between assessment for learning (formative) and assessment of learning (summative), as each serves a different purpose in supporting progress. Below are the features of the different types of assessment.

Formative assessment (assessment *for* learning):

- is ongoing, informal and embedded within daily teaching
- helps teachers make immediate adjustments to lessons based on pupil responses
- includes strategies such as questioning, mini whiteboard responses, self-assessment, peer assessment and classroom discussions.

Summative assessment (assessment of learning):

- is typically used at the end of a unit, term or year to evaluate overall learning
- provides a snapshot of attainment but does not always capture a pupil's full mathematical understanding
- includes tests such as SATs, termly assessments and standardised maths papers.

Both types of assessment are valuable, but formative assessment should be prioritised in daily practice. It has the most direct impact on learning, as it allows teachers to respond to pupils' needs in real time. Summative assessments are useful for tracking long-term progress.

Using assessment to support learning

Assessment in maths should not be seen as the final step in learning but as a continuous process that informs teaching and supports pupil progress. In maths, this means using day-to-day evidence, such as pupil explanations, whiteboard responses or reasoning discussions, to adapt instruction in real time. When used effectively, assessment provides valuable insights that enable teachers to address misconceptions early, adjust the level of challenge and ensure secure understanding before moving on.

Black and Wiliam (1998) argue that assessment should be primarily formative, used to enhance learning rather than just measure attainment. For maths leaders, this involves developing a culture of responsive teaching. This might mean modelling to their colleagues how to use mini-whiteboards to gather instant responses during a fluency session, how to interpret exit tickets to identify pupils who need additional support with reasoning tasks or how to encourage pupils to streamline and refine their verbal explanations before writing them down. Encouraging teachers to treat every question, misconception or pupil explanation as assessment evidence can transform how teaching decisions are made.

Providing meaningful feedback

Feedback is one of the most effective ways to improve pupil learning (Hattie & Timperley, 2007). However, for feedback to be impactful, it must be timely, specific and actionable. In maths, this means focusing feedback on how pupils are thinking, not just whether they arrived at the correct answer. Key principles of effective feedback in maths include:

- focusing on process, not just outcome – instead of simply marking an answer as right or wrong, effective feedback highlights the reasoning behind a mistake and guides pupils towards improvement. For example, when adding fractions with the same denominators, a teacher could say 'I can see you have added the numerators and denominators here. What happens to the denominator when we add fractions with the same denominator?'
- encouraging self-reflection – pupils should be given opportunities to respond to feedback, correct their work, and reflect on their understanding. For example, a teacher might ask 'What do you notice about your method? Can you correct this one using the method we practised yesterday?'
- providing scaffolding rather than solutions – rather than telling pupils the correct answer, feedback should prompt them to think more deeply. For example, when looking at cubing numbers, a teacher might prompt by saying 'You've multiplied 8 by 3 here. What does the 3 represent when we cube numbers?'.

Addressing misconceptions

Misconceptions in maths are not just errors; they're evidence of partial understanding. If left unaddressed, they can compound over time, particularly in areas like place value, fractions and the four operations. Effective formative assessment helps teachers identify these misconceptions early, turning them into learning opportunities.

Dylan Wiliam (2011) argues that assessment should be used diagnostically to uncover why pupils are making errors. Harry Fletcher-Wood (2018) extends this through the use of hinge questions, which are carefully designed checks that reveal whether pupils have grasped key concepts before moving on.

In practice: example hinge questions

EYFS

Concept: Understanding the cardinal value of a number.

Hinge Question: I have counted these five counters: 1, 2, 3, 4, 5. So, how many are there altogether?

Options:

a) 4
b) 5
c) 6
d) I don't know

Given the age of pupils in EYFS, this sort of question would be part of a small group activity focusing on counting objects in front of them and the children would give their answers verbally.

KS1

Concept: Understanding the inverse relationship between addition and subtraction.

Hinge Question: Which number sentence could help you solve 14 – 6 = ?

Options:

a) 14 + 6 = ?
b) 6 + ? = 14
c) 14 – ? = 6
d) 6 – 14 = ?

LKS2

Concept: Place value understanding in decimals.

Hinge Question: Which of these numbers is the same as 4.09?

Options:

a) Four and nine tenths
b) Four and nine hundredths
c) Forty and nine hundredths
d) Four and ninety hundredths

UKS2

Concept: Understanding the properties of shape – angles in a triangle.

Hinge Question: A triangle has two angles of 40° and 60°. What is the third angle?

Options:

a) 40°
b) 60°
c) 80°
d) 100°

Misconceptions should be addressed through targeted interventions, small-group discussions, and guided re-teaching of concepts. Providing opportunities for pupils to confront and resolve misunderstandings leads to long-term retention and conceptual understanding (Skemp, 1976).

Planning next steps

Assessment is not an endpoint. In maths, assessment should lead directly into action. The purpose of collecting assessment information, whether from a quiz, observation or end-of-unit task, is to inform what teachers do next. Using assessment to plan next steps involves several key approaches.

- Identifying gaps: After an assessment, teachers should analyse patterns in pupil responses to determine which concepts need revisiting.
- Adapting instruction: Pupils who demonstrate secure understanding may be ready for further challenge and enrichment, while those who struggle may need scaffolding or corrective teaching.

- Incorporating retrieval practice: Key learning points identified in assessments should be revisited at spaced intervals to strengthen retention (Roediger & Butler, 2011).

For example, if an assessment reveals that many pupils struggle with fractions, the teacher might take the following steps.

1. Adjust upcoming lessons to include additional fluency practice with fraction equivalence.
2. Introduce concrete representations (e.g. fraction strips) to reinforce conceptual understanding.
3. Set low-stakes quizzes that revisit fractions across the next half-term to prevent forgetting.

At a whole-school level, you can support staff in using assessment to inform planning. You can:

1. agree the assessment focus and what 'secure' looks like for this concept
2. use a mix of formative and summative assessment to gather information
3. analyse the outcomes and look for patterns, such as common errors or misunderstood vocabulary
4. pinpoint specific misconceptions that pupils have
5. respond to assessment by planning to re-teach content, embedding content in retrieval practice or using targeted intervention
6. plan for re-assessment after the above
7. evaluate the impact of what you did.

Making assessment data meaningful

Simply collecting numbers and tracking scores without a clear purpose can lead to an over-reliance on data without real impact on teaching and learning. In maths, your role is to ensure that assessment data is used meaningfully, guiding teacher decisions, shaping interventions and supporting school improvement. You can do this by working alongside your SLT or the assessment lead to unpick what the data is telling you.

Interpreting assessment data

Data analysis in maths is most effective when it is focused, collaborative and directly informs future teaching (Wiliam, 2011). The aim isn't to analyse every single point but to identify key trends that have implications for next steps, such as misconceptions about fractions, persistent difficulties with word problems or uneven progress across strands, e.g. geometry and measure. The following are steps for analysing maths data effectively.

- First, ask where this assessment has come from and if it is accurate. You might ask: Where did the questions come from and were they aligned with what was taught? Was the assessment accessible to all pupils? Were the conditions consistent across classes? Are the results fairly consistent with what we already know? Was the marking accurate and consistent?
- Look for patterns across year groups and phases to check for common areas where multiple pupils are struggling, or for particular question types that highlight gaps in reasoning skills.
- Stiggins (2002) highlights the importance of triangulating assessment data, using a combination of tests, classroom observations and pupil discussions to ensure a complete picture of understanding. Compare performance across different assessments.

Discuss findings with teachers in pupil progress meetings. Boudett et al. (2013) argue that using simple visual representations, such as colour-coded spreadsheets and clear diagrams, makes data more actionable for teachers. Share accessible data in small, focused meetings rather than overwhelming teachers with lots of percentages. You might compare data from end of unit tests with data from end of term tests. Encourage teachers to reflect on what the data tells them about their class's understanding, and work together to agree on practical next steps in response to the data.

Using assessment to inform intervention

One valuable use of data is identifying where pupils may need additional support. Effective interventions are timely, targeted and directly linked to classroom teaching. The following are some considerations for assessment-driven interventions.

- Short, focused interventions are more effective than lengthy ones: Sweller's CLT suggests that pupils learn best in small, manageable steps rather than long, complex sessions (1988). You might decide to break up an intervention into three 15 minute sessions rather than one single long session.
- Flexible grouping supports individual needs: Sherrington (2019) warns against rigid ability grouping, arguing that pupils benefit from fluid intervention groups based on specific learning gaps rather than fixed attainment levels. Instead of having fixed groups that pupils work in for maths lessons, I find it is more effective to seat pupils based on personality, mixing up prior attainment, to get the best out of them. Then, if there are pupils who need more focused attention in a lesson, you can pull them together to work with them.
- Same-day 'keep up' sessions can be a powerful strategy informed by formative assessment. If pupils are self-marking, teachers can find five minutes either at the end of a lesson or before the afternoon lessons start to flick through the books and check if anyone needs a post-teaching session to re-teach the concept or have more time practising the core concept before the next lesson.

As a maths subject leader, you can model this approach in staff meetings or lesson study sessions, showing how quick, targeted intervention can prevent small misconceptions from growing into larger barriers.

Balancing numbers with professional judgement

While tracking numerical data is essential, it should never replace teacher expertise. Maths assessment must balance quantitative evidence with qualitative insight – what teachers know from observing pupil reasoning, discussions and representations. Stobart (2008) warns that over-reliance on test scores can lead to distorted teaching priorities, where teachers focus on 'teaching to the test' rather than deep understanding. The following are some principles for balancing data with teacher judgement.

- Context matters: Black & Wiliam (2018) argue that test scores can be affected by factors such as anxiety, test format and prior experiences. This means teachers must consider pupil confidence, engagement and classroom performance alongside data.
- Formative assessment is more predictive of learning than summative alone: Hattie (2009) found that formative assessment strategies, such

as questioning, retrieval practice and real-time feedback, have a greater impact on progress than summative assessments alone.

- Teacher judgement is invaluable: Christodoulou (2017) highlights the importance of combining teacher expertise with data, as teachers can interpret errors in context. For example, a pupil might struggle with fractions due to a misconception about division, not fractions themselves.

Questions for reflection

- How well does assessment in our school support learning rather than just measure attainment?
- Are our teachers confident in using both formative and summative assessments effectively?
- Do assessments in our school accurately reflect conceptual understanding, or do they primarily assess procedural fluency?
- How does our school use assessment data to inform interventions?
- What steps can we take to ensure assessment is manageable, purposeful and not an unnecessary burden on staff or pupils?
- How do we ensure that assessments are accessible and fair for pupils with SEND or those learning EAL?

Example PD session: developing use of formative assessment

Here is an example of what a PD session on formative assessment could look like.

TIMING SUGGESTION	SESSION GUIDANCE
5 mins	• Recap formative and summative assessment. Most teachers will be able to articulate the difference and give examples, but it's good practice to retrieve the relevant information before using it in the rest of the meeting. • Highlight the importance of using formative assessment (e.g. questioning, discussions and mini whiteboards) to guide teaching in real time and support pupil learning. • Explain that the session will focus on practical strategies for using formative assessment to identify gaps and misconceptions and plan next steps in teaching.

TIMING SUGGESTION	SESSION GUIDANCE
10 mins	• Give an overview of the key functions of formative assessment: identifying gaps, adjusting teaching and offering immediate feedback. • Share research findings from Hattie & Timperley (2007) and Wiliam & Leahy (2015) about how formative assessment improves learning. Hattie & Timperley (2007) found that the impact of feedback varies. Feedback that focuses on the task that directs pupils on where to go next is most effective, whereas feedback focusing on praise and rewards shows less impact. Wiliam & Leahy (2015) shared formative assessment strategies, such as sharing and clarifying learning intentions, engineering tasks that elicit evidence of learning and providing feedback that moves forward. • Show how formative assessments (e.g. hinge questions) can reveal misconceptions early on. • Have a whole-group discussion on how teachers currently use formative assessment in their classrooms, and what kinds of assessments they use to gauge pupils' understanding during a lesson.

15 mins	• Share examples of the following techniques for formative assessment.
	    • Questioning: Using open-ended and probing questions to check for understanding.
	    • Mini whiteboards: Allowing pupils to display their thinking quickly.
	    • Peer-/self-assessment: Encouraging pupils to assess their own or each other's work to promote reflection. Exit tickets: Holding a quick, informal assessment at the end of the lesson.
	    • Targeted feedback: Giving verbal or written feedback that guides improvement and encourages pupils to act on it.
	• Discuss when to use each of these techniques. Consider what output you are trying to get from each one.
	• In pairs, teachers create examples of formative assessments they could use in their own classrooms based on what is coming up next.
	• Share some examples with the group.

TIMING SUGGESTION	SESSION GUIDANCE
15 mins	• Discuss the importance of identifying misconceptions and how they can persist if not addressed immediately. • Use an example of a common misconception in maths, such as a misinterpretation of place value in addition and subtraction and show how formative assessments can uncover this early. • Discuss the role of hinge questions in checking for misconceptions at critical points in a lesson. • Share a misconception related to a maths concept and discuss how you might use formative assessment to uncover and address it. An example misconception could be that when adding using the column method, a pupil puts 11 in the ones column instead of regrouping/exchanging 11 ones for one ten and one one. You could use a short set of multiple-choice questions and mini whiteboards to test whether pupils make that mistake. Then, you could get out the place value counters to model and practise physically regrouping/exchanging. • Ask teachers to work in pairs or small groups to come up with a specific misconception for their subject area and share how they would address it through formative assessment.

10 mins	• Highlight the principles of effective feedback:
	  • Focus on the process, not just the outcome.
	  • Encourage pupils to reflect on their learning.
	  • Provide scaffolding for further development rather than just giving answers.
	• Discuss how formative assessment data can inform instructional decisions, identify gaps, enrich learning and challenge pupils who are ready. For example, if pupils are struggling with fractions, use formative assessment data to adjust upcoming lessons (e.g. to revisit equivalent fractions or use concrete resources).
	• Discuss how teachers currently use formative assessment to plan next steps. Ask them to think about a recent lesson and how formative assessment data could have informed their next steps.

5 mins	• Encourage teachers to reflect on the session's learning and consider how they might apply formative assessment strategies in their own classrooms. • Action step: Teachers to choose one strategy they will implement in the next week (e.g. using hinge questions, mini whiteboards or peer assessment).

Explore further

- *Making Good Progress? The Future of Assessment for Learning* (2017) by Daisy Christodoulou
- *Embedded Formative Assessment* (2011) by Dylan Wiliam
- The EEF's guidance report *Teacher Feedback to Improve Pupil Learning* (2021) by Joe Collin and Alex Quigley: https://files.eric.ed.gov/fulltext/ED615988.pdf
- *Tackling Misconceptions in Primary Mathematics* (2016) by Kieran Mackle

Chapter summary

- Assessment should measure teaching impact, identify gaps and inform next steps.
- A combination of formative and summative approaches ensures a fuller understanding of pupil progress.
- Assessments should be judged on their validity, reliability, accessibility, breadth and depth.
- Feedback should be timely, specific and actionable to help pupils improve.
- Addressing misconceptions is key to preventing persistent errors.
- Data should guide responsive teaching and targeted interventions while being balanced with teacher judgement.
- Assessment should empower teachers, not overwhelm them.

12 Writing (and using) purposeful maths policies

Developing, refining and embedding policies is a significant part of your role as the maths subject leader. A well-crafted maths policy brings together vision and practice, articulating not only what teachers do, but why they do it. This chapter will explore the purpose of polices in primary maths, how consistency and uniformity play a part in policy design and a process for building a strong policy.

Why policies matter in primary maths

The primary purpose of a maths policy is to create coherence, ensuring that pupils have a high-quality, joined-up experience of maths from EYFS to Year 6. It helps teachers understand how the school approaches curriculum sequencing, pedagogy, assessment and inclusion.

A clear, living policy is one of the highest-leverage tools you have as the primary maths subject leader. Policies turn values into practice, reduce avoidable inconsistency and help everyone make better day-to-day decisions. Good policies share the purpose of what we're trying to achieve for pupils, make the minimum expectations clear to readers and protect professional judgement where teachers can make informed decisions to adapt the policy for their class.

Consistency and uniformity

When writing or refining policy, you might find it helpful to distinguish between consistency and uniformity.

Consistency means shared principles and agreed practices that support progression and pupil understanding. For example, using agreed models such as part-whole diagrams and bar models across the school or everyone checking for understanding routinely in lessons. Consistency in policies aims for the same level of high-quality teaching and learning without demanding identical practice.

Uniformity refers to surface-level sameness, for example, everyone using the same-coloured books for maths across the school or using short titles over long learning objectives. When taken too far, uniformity can stifle teacher agency and professional judgement. The key is to be deliberate: every uniform expectation should have a clear rationale that links back to improving teaching and learning.

Updating your policy

A maths policy shouldn't be a document that gathers dust. It should guide classroom practice, be revisited regularly and evolve as understanding and priorities develop. In most schools, this does not mean constant change. Instead, policies might be formally reviewed annually, with smaller refinements made at key points across the year (for example, following a unit, a term or a professional development cycle). The aim is stability with responsiveness, not frequent change that creates additional workload.

Frequent change can quickly undermine confidence and consistency, so it is important that policies feel stable for teachers. Refinement should be purposeful and based on evidence, not continual rewriting.

In reality, policy writing rarely feels neat and tidy. You might be working with inherited documents from a previous subject leader or you might be grappling with balancing different staff views or trying to refine practice without overwhelming your team. I have found myself rewriting policies, wondering whether they will actually make a difference in classrooms. The most important shift for me was moving away from writing policies for compliance and towards writing them as tools that genuinely support teachers' day-to-day decisions. If a policy doesn't help a teacher at 10:15am on a Wednesday, it probably needs changing. You have to ask yourself 'Who is this policy for?'

What a maths policy might cover

1 Planning and pedagogy

Aim: To ensure maths lessons are coherent, well-sequenced and responsive to pupils' understanding. A maths policy might include:

- use of long-term and medium-term curriculum maps aligned to the National Curriculum in England
- expectation that lessons follow a clear structure
- use of formative assessment to check understanding before moving on
- emphasis on CPA progression and connections between representations
- expectation that reasoning and problem solving are embedded regularly, not taught as stand-alone lessons
- opportunities for teachers to adapt planning for class need while maintaining curriculum intent.

2 Exercise books (or alternatives)

Aim: To provide a clear, consistent record of pupils' mathematical thinking and progression over time. A maths policy might include:

- phase-appropriate book type
- expectations for layout and presentation
- efficient sharing and/or recording of learning objectives
- clarity around use of jottings, annotations and representations to show thinking
- recording expectations for EYFS
- emphasis on content quality and evidence of reasoning over handwriting or neatness alone.

3 Representations and models

Aim: To ensure pupils encounter and use consistent, high-quality representations that expose mathematical structure and deepen understanding. A maths policy might include:

- a school-wide progression map showing which core models are introduced and revisited in each year group
- expectation that new models are explicitly taught and connected to prior representations
- use of multiple representations for key concepts
- guidance on when to move between concrete, pictorial and abstract forms
- examples of how to model reasoning using representations

- flexibility for teachers to choose additional representations based on pupil need once core ones are secure.

4 Grouping

Aim: To promote inclusive, flexible approaches that support all pupils in accessing and achieving success in maths. A maths policy might include:

- a whole-class teaching approach as the default (in line with mastery approaches and Maths Hubs guidance), with scaffolds and extensions used within lessons
- use of flexible grouping informed by formative assessment, not fixed 'ability' groups
- clear guidance on when and how same-day or targeted intervention should take place
- expectation that every pupil experiences challenge and depth before acceleration
- consideration of SEND and EAL needs, with adaptation rather than reduction of challenge.

5 Displays and working walls

Aim: To provide evolving visual supports that make current learning, language and models visible and usable for pupils. A maths policy might include:

- a clear distinction between fixed displays (celebration) and working walls (live learning)
- inclusion of current vocabulary, sentence stems and key representations
- use of live, co-created worked examples rather than static, pre-printed materials
- regular updates as new concepts are taught
- accessibility principles
- encouragement for teachers to use walls interactively in lessons.

6 Task Design

Aim: To ensure mathematical tasks provide appropriate practice, challenge and opportunities for reasoning and problem solving. A maths policy might include:

- shared task design principles: variation; low-threshold, high-ceiling; purposeful practice
- balance of fluency, reasoning and problem-solving tasks within each unit
- expectation that tasks move from guided to independent practice
- use of intelligent variation sequences
- guidance on when and how to use manipulatives or scaffolds
- example banks of high-quality tasks aligned to curriculum objectives.

7 Assessment

Aim: To gather valid, reliable and meaningful evidence of mathematical understanding that informs teaching and supports pupil progress. A maths policy might include:

- use of formative assessment strategies in every lesson
- agreed summative assessment points
- common end-of-unit/term assessment materials for comparability
- guidance on using data diagnostically to identify misconceptions and plan next steps
- moderation processes to ensure consistency in teacher judgement
- recording expectations and how outcomes are shared with pupils and parents.

How long should your policy be?

A policy for teachers should be as user-friendly as possible. This means it shouldn't be tens of pages long with paragraphs of endless text because this is hard to navigate and hard to put into practice. On the flip side, very short policies can be too vague and open to interpretation. A helpful test is whether a teacher can quickly find and apply the guidance during planning or teaching. If not, the policy may need tweaking. Consider using visuals, bullet points, key words in bold and one topic per page so that teachers can easily find the section they need.

A simple process for building strong maths policies

1 Diagnose

- Consider the problem that you need to solve.
- Look at the evidence of current practice.

2 Draft

- Clarify the intent of the policy.
- Define the active ingredients needed to fulfil the intent.
- Outline the underlying consistent principles.
- Decide what should be uniform and what can be adapted.

3 Consult

- Share a one-page working draft with key stakeholders.
- Discuss the practical implications, advantages and constraints of the policy.
- Revise for clarity and workload.

4 Pilot

- Plan a small-scale trial of the policy for an agreed amount of time.
- Collect evidence of the policy along the way.

5 Implement

- Launch with high-quality professional development.
- Provide a one-page guide with exemplars.
- Give staff time to plan how to enact the policy.

6 Evaluate

- Use low-stakes evaluation activities focused on how well the policy serves learning.
- Deploy coaches to work with staff on the policy.
- Continue to evaluate the impact and refine the policy over time.

After this process, teachers should understand which aspects are non-negotiable because they support learning and progression, and which aspects allow for professional discretion because they depend on pupils, context or teacher expertise. Teachers should also be able to see that the policy is not entirely set in stone and is subject to ongoing evaluation and refinement.

Case study: using the process to build a strong policy

Sophie is the maths leader at a two-form-entry primary school in the Midlands. She has used the above process to create, implement and embed a new policy.

1 Diagnose

When Sophie begins as maths leader, she notices that pupils are using very different models and manipulatives depending on who teaches them. In Year 2, pupils use ten frames and bead strings but by Year 4, they are expected to interpret bar models they have never seen before. Lesson visits reveal that some teachers use representations daily, while others prefer abstract methods from the outset. To better understand the issue, Sophie conducts:

- book looks across all year groups to identify which models are being used and how consistently
- pupil voice interviews asking children which models help them and which confuse them
- teacher surveys to find out which representations staff feel confident using and where they need support.

The findings show that while teachers value manipulatives and visual models, there is no shared progression or rationale guiding their use. This inconsistency is limiting pupils' ability to make connections across topics and year groups.

2 Draft

Sophie begins drafting a Representations and Models Policy to address the inconsistency while protecting teacher autonomy.

She settles on the intent: To ensure that pupils experience a consistent and coherent journey in the use of mathematical representations, building deep conceptual understanding and independence in choosing models to support their thinking. Then, she begins thinking about active ingredients:

- Each year group introduces and revisits core representations (defined in a school-wide progression map).
- Teachers explicitly link new models to previously taught ones.
- Concrete, pictorial and abstract representations are interwoven throughout teaching sequences.

Sophie decides that a consistent principle of the policy should be that representations must expose mathematical structure, reduce cognitive load and support reasoning. She drafts an example set of core representations, including part–whole models, number lines, place value counters and bar models. In the draft policy, Sophie acknowledges that teachers know their pupils best, so understand how they might tweak the contexts, visuals and manipulatives to meet the needs of different pupils.

3 Consult

Sophie shares a one-page working draft with key stakeholders: year group leads, the SENDCo and two Early Career Teachers. During a short after-school meeting, they discuss:

- practicality: can teachers access the manipulatives needed?
- progression: are the chosen models developmentally appropriate?
- workload: how can the policy reduce planning time rather than add to it?

Staff appreciate the clarity and simplicity but suggest adding:

- photographic exemplars of the models in use
- explicit guidance on introducing new manipulatives to pupils.
- Sophie incorporates these ideas and reduces the written policy to two concise pages with clear visuals.

4 Pilot

Sophie runs a six-week pilot in Years 3 and 4, focusing on fractions and multiplication structures.

Teachers use the agreed models (bar model, array and number line) in lessons, upload annotated lesson slides and photos of pupils' work to a shared drive and reflect weekly in a ten minute catch-up led by Sophie.

Sophie collects evidence, including samples of pupils' books showing bar models, arrays and number lines, and teacher reflections on what supports or hinders understanding.

The pilot shows that pupils quickly recognise links between models, for example seeing arrays and bar models as both showing multiplication structures. Teachers report that pupils are more confident in choosing representations independently.

5 Implement

After refining the policy, Sophie launches it for the whole school during a staff meeting. The session includes:

- a short input on the rationale
- a visual progression map showing when and how each model should be introduced
- hands-on professional development where staff explore manipulatives and match them to lesson objectives
- a one-page guide for classroom reference, including photographs, model progressions and sentence stems for linking representations.

Teachers are given time at the end of the session to plan their next unit using the new progression map, noting where they would explicitly connect representations.

Sophie then does a shorter input two weeks later in another PD meeting so that teachers can have a refresher and ask any questions that have come up since her initial session.

6 Evaluate

Over the next term, Sophie evaluates the policy's impact through: low-stakes learning walks focused on how models are being used, not on compliance; pupil interviews asking 'Which models help you understand new maths?'; and teacher drop-ins where Sophie coaches staff on linking models to abstract notation.

Teachers report higher confidence and less planning time spent searching for resources. However, pupil explanations still lack the focus on mathematical structure that Sophie is aiming for. She uses the evidence from her evaluation activities to inform her next steps in refining the policy. Sophie plans another PD session focusing purely on mathematical structure, and works with phase leaders and the SENDCo on how to refine the policy further to include this.

Example PD session: introducing a new policy

Here is an example of what a PD session on introducing a new policy could look like. It could be adapted to suit any policy.

TIMING SUGGESTION	**SESSION GUIDANCE**
5 mins	• Begin with a quote or pupil voice snippet that captures why the policy was needed. • Outline the purpose of the policy.
10 mins	• Share the evidence that led to the policy change, for example snapshots from book looks, lesson visits, staff feedback or pupil responses. • Ask the staff what problems they have noticed relating to this policy area. • Ask them to discuss the policy in pairs, then share one key challenge that the policy aims to address.
15 mins	• Present the intent of the policy and the active ingredients. • Use an example to make the policy more concrete for staff. • Highlight the consistent underlying principles. In small groups, discuss why these shouldn't change. • Explain which parts should feel uniform across the board with a surface level sameness, and why this sameness is beneficial to pupil learning. • Share what can be adapted based on the context and the knowledge teachers have of their classes.

TIMING SUGGESTION	SESSION GUIDANCE
20 mins	• Split the group into phase or year group teams depending on the number of staff. Give each group a short maths objective that links to an upcoming area of study for that phase or year group. • Ask the groups to discuss this objective through the lens of the new policy and its principles. Ask them to consider the impact of the policy on pupil learning. • Give the groups paper to record their ideas.
15 mins	• Give each group some time to present their objective and thoughts. • Invite peer feedback and debate. • Highlight and reinforce the connections to the policy principles after each group.
5 mins	• Ask staff to complete a quick reflection related to the policy. • Ask each teacher to consider what the policy will look like in their classroom in the next week, term and for the rest of the year. • Give each teacher a sticky note to write an action for themselves, and stick this on a 'commitment' board or poster.
5 mins	• Summarise the key takeaways from the policy and the discussions. • Share how the policy will be supported and evaluated in the coming weeks. • End with a pupil-focused reminder so that staff leave with the memory of the impact on pupil learning.

Questions for reflection

- What current policies in my school genuinely support teaching and learning in maths, and which might exist more for compliance?
- How well do our existing maths policies distinguish between consistency (shared principles) and uniformity (surface-level sameness)?
- When writing or revising a policy, how can I make sure that the 'why' is clear to all staff?
- Who should I involve in consultation to make the policy both workable and well-understood?
- What might a small-scale pilot look like in my context before a full implementation?

- How can I build opportunities for low-stakes evaluation and refinement of the policy over time?
- How will I ensure that professional development focuses on practice and not just policy awareness?
- In what ways can I celebrate and share examples of the policy in action to build momentum and confidence across staff?

Explore further

- *Thinking Deeply about Primary Mathematics* (2020) by Kieran Mackle
- *How I Wish I'd Taught Maths* (2018) by Craig Barton

Chapter summary

- A well-written maths policy translates the school's vision into clear, practical action that improves learning for pupils.
- Policies are most effective when they balance consistency of principles with flexibility in practice, allowing teachers to exercise professional judgement.
- Every uniform expectation should have a clear rationale linked to pupil understanding or teacher efficiency, never compliance for its own sake.
- Strong policies focus on intent (the 'why') and active ingredients (the 'what' that drives impact).
- Developing a policy is a process (diagnose, draft, consult, pilot, implement, evaluate) and not a one-off event.
- Professional development should focus on bringing the policy to life through practical application, not just presentation.
- Ongoing evaluation ensures that policies evolve alongside staff expertise and the changing needs of pupils.

13 Implementing change

As a maths leader, you'll be tasked with making changes, whether it's improving fluency, embedding a new scheme, developing reasoning or increasing staff confidence. You will almost definitely be asked to write an action plan for maths. Making change stick is about more than putting good ideas in a document. It's about thoughtful, phased implementation. A key tool for this is the EEF's guidance on implementation (2024), which we will work through in this chapter to help you implement maths improvement with clarity and confidence.

Why planning implementation matters

Introducing change in a school can feel deceptively straightforward: identify a problem, pick a solution, roll it out. But any school or subject leader knows that real, lasting improvement is rarely this linear. Too often, well-intentioned initiatives fade into the background, crowded out by other priorities, misunderstood by staff or undermined by inconsistent delivery. That's where implementation planning becomes crucial.

Strong implementation isn't just about launching a new idea; it's about embedding it into the fabric of teaching and learning. It requires time, clarity, collaboration and responsiveness. Without a structured approach, even the most evidence-informed, promising changes risk becoming 'another thing we tried once'.

When implementation is carefully planned, three things happen:

1. People understand the purpose.
2. The process is manageable.
3. The change sticks.

A maths leader who plans well creates the conditions for teachers to succeed and for pupils to benefit. This doesn't require complex project management tools, but it does require intention, alignment and follow-through.

Common pitfalls in implementing change

Bringing about meaningful change is rarely a smooth or simple process. In our drive to make improvements, we sometimes rush into introducing new initiatives without thinking through how they'll be put into practice or what support is needed to give them the best chance of success. Too often, key questions like who will lead the work, why it matters, where and when it will happen and how it will be sustained are not given enough attention. As a result, even well-meaning changes can lose momentum or fail entirely, especially in busy school environments where priorities are constantly competing. Understanding that implementation is a complex process can help school leaders to be more resilient, recognising that obstacles are not signs of failure but normal parts of the change process. Here are some of the most common mistakes seen in schools:

- rushing to act before understanding the problem
- trying to implement too many things at once
- introducing too much, too soon
- subject priorities not aligning with school improvement priorities
- confusing communication
- lack of follow-up
- no plan for sustainability
- lack of time given to implementation activities
- introducing something that isn't based on what the school needs.

The EEF's implementation guidance report

In 2024, the Education Endowment Foundation published an updated guidance report titled *Putting Evidence to Work: A School's Guide to Implementation*. The guidance reminds us that success is never just about having a good idea – it's about putting that idea into practice in the right way. It is a practical, evidence-based framework designed to help schools plan, deliver and sustain effective change.

The report begins with the context. Before anything is set in motion, leaders need to reflect on three essential questions:

- What exactly are we trying to implement?
- Do we have the systems and structures to make it work?
- Do we have the right people to lead and influence the process?

The first question asks us to check whether the approach is informed by sound evidence, whether it is right for our school's setting and whether it is genuinely feasible to put into action. The second reminds us that change needs an infrastructure to succeed, for example clear roles, allocated time and practical logistics. The third points to the importance of people: champions and leaders who can guide, support and inspire others through the journey.

Once the context is understood, the EEF describes implementation as a cycle with four interconnected stages: Explore, Prepare, Deliver, Sustain. These are discussed in more detail later on in the chapter.

Running through the whole process are three core behaviours that keep implementation alive and effective: Engage, Unite, Reflect.

Engage requires involving people so they can shape what happens, while still keeping a clear sense of direction. Unite is building a shared understanding of what is being implemented, how it will be done and why it matters, so that all stakeholders have buy-in. Finally, Reflect requires evaluating progress, learning from experience and making changes where needed to improve the outcome.

The power of the EEF's model lies in the way these elements work together. The context shapes the choices we make, the process gives us a map to follow and the behaviours keep everyone connected and moving in the same direction. When all three come together, schools give themselves the best chance of turning good ideas into lasting, meaningful improvement.

We will look at the key recommendations in the EEF's implementation guidance and explore a case study for each part. The focus of the case study will be embedding a reasoning progression framework across KS1 and KS2 maths lessons.

1. Adopt the behaviours that drive effective implementation

Successful implementation isn't just about following steps. It relies heavily on how people behave during the process. As a maths subject leader, modelling the behaviours that promote strong implementation is key. This includes being deliberate, persistent and proactive in your leadership. Rather than rushing to put new strategies in place, take time to diagnose what your school needs and make thoughtful decisions based on evidence.

One of the most powerful behaviours is creating buy-in. Instead of simply telling teachers what needs to change, invite them into the process. Share the rationale behind your decisions, listen to their concerns, and work collaboratively to shape a shared vision. With your fellow leaders, you can build a culture of trust and psychological safety that allows staff to feel confident trying new approaches and reflecting openly on what is and isn't working.

Another important behaviour is prioritisation. It's easy to want to do everything at once, especially when there are so many areas of maths we could improve, but implementation is more successful when we focus our energy on doing fewer things well. Choose one or two high-leverage areas to work on and do them thoroughly before moving on. Behaving in ways that promote clarity, responsiveness and collaboration will help secure long-term change.

Interview on times table mastery – Grahame MacMullen

Grahame is a trust maths curriculum lead and an NCETM Mastery Specialist. He has developed a suite of resources for times table teaching across his multi-academy trust.

Q: What inspired you to make these resources?

A: I was training as an NCETM Mastery Specialist, so I was thinking about the Big Ideas of mastery. The NCETM fluency idea is not just accurate recall, but also the ability to understand quickly what those facts mean, how they are related to each other and being able to apply them in different ways. I had a project to do as part of my training, and I thought, 'I need something that's going to allow me to work on all these ideas with the teachers in my school'. I watched an Ofsted video about what times table practice should be like, and it asked 'What system do you have to allow you to teach times tables?'. I thought, 'Do we have a system?'. I spoke to teachers in Year 5 and 6 who said that one of the things that holds children back is not knowing their times table facts. It underpins so much of the curriculum. So much of it is based on multiplicative thinking and to be fluent with your multiplication facts. So, I started to look at what systems or approaches were out there. Nothing really did what we wanted it to do, so I thought perhaps we needed to create our own system.

Q: How did you go about that?

A: My first step was to see what was happening in our Year 2, 3 and 4 classes. What systems were already being used? We had lots of teachers doing good work, but we didn't have a coherent system with progression that was enabling every child to learn their times tables. We had good practice in different year groups and classes, but we needed a school-wide progression. I thought very carefully about it because it was obviously going to be quite a big investment of my time, and I wondered whether it would be worth it and if it would make a big difference. If we could ensure that all children were going to learn their times tables, that would make a big difference to their learning. We didn't want to have a system that was just parroting facts without a depth of understanding, or without children being able to reason, connect and understand the meaning of those facts and how they connect all the ideas around multiplication.

Q: When you started creating those resources, how did you structure it?

A: I used Debbie Morgan's Big Ideas from the NCETM. They have been incredibly influential. I find it hard to imagine planning and working on maths without those things now. Therefore, I had that model in front of me. We need to start with using representations that will reveal the structure of the mathematics. So, I thought about what representations we needed and where I was going to start. We started this in Year 3. These are children in a very early stage of starting to learn about multiplication and their times tables. They've done a bit of work in Year 2, and what I must not do is assume that they already have a really good understanding of the very basic idea of multiplication being the repeated addition of the same number. I thought, 'What is going to be the clearest way to represent this? What visual representations are they going to have, and what language am I going to use to scaffold understanding for all of the children to be able to access their curriculum?'. I thought about the kind of representations that we would need, and I decided to start with an array. I wanted to have a system which involved a lot of mathematical thinking. I wanted it to be quite interactive, and I wanted to work in small steps. I didn't want the children's working memory to be overloaded at any point, instead it progresses with a very consistent structure in small steps of learning.

At all times, children are trying to think and explain. They have opportunities to draw and record. I thought carefully about how we keep our language consistent, and then over time, how we vary the representations. So, after an array, we go on to a number line, but we show the groups of three on that array because they have moved on to the number line, and then we can see the jumps on the number line. After that, we have other important representations. We start to see three as Numicon, where it already unitised. Then, we start to see a bar model. I kept the bar model near the end because in some ways, it's the most abstract; it's important that we don't jump onto abstract things too early in the progression. I also wanted to have a mixture of opportunities to practise in school, so we needed a system whereby the children were regularly testing themselves, but wasn't just a testing system. They needed to learn, think, understand and reason. There were opportunities to retrieve and practise so the pupils strengthen their recall over time. It was important to me that we teach and practise the tables in school, so that we don't over rely on support at home. Our disadvantaged children would suffer the most because they won't necessarily have the same levels of support in many cases. It's about equity. I am really passionate that every child gets a chance through their education.

It's not just down to parents and carers/families. It's down to us as teachers. A fundamental thing is that if we're offering a system, then it has to work for the children at school.

Q: How did you find time to fit in the new teaching?

A: I was keen to not ask for more time in the school week. The timetable is already very busy. We're trying to teach a broad and balanced curriculum; therefore, we decided that we weren't going to have to ask people to spend less time on other things. I wasn't going to ask everyone to find extra time every day or week, but I did ask them to put aside half of one maths lesson a week. So, it became one half an hour session per week and then five minutes either at the start or the end of every maths lesson. I thought that was really important, and you have to consider your impact across the curriculum. Realistically, it means we are teaching less of the curriculum each week, but what we have found is that by starting to teach times tables in this systematic way from the start of Year 3, a lot of the topics go much quicker when you get on to them. So, if you invest some time at the start, then all the work that you do later on in the scheme using multiplication, division, fractions, decimals and percentages goes much better and more quickly.

Q: How did you introduce the resources to staff?

A: I wrote one set of resources myself for the three times table, and I asked my Year 3 colleagues if they would mind me coming down every Thursday morning to do a 20-25 minute session with their class. They were very happy for me to come down because they had realised we needed a more consistent model. By teaching the new sessions to both Year 3 classes, I was able to model to the teachers and trial this new consistent set of resources. Essentially, we started with a trial in our Year 3 classes for a half term. The teachers played an important role in feeding back because it's important for them to value the resources and see the impact. We saw an improvement in that first half term because the children were really fluent with their threes. We did an assessment at the end of the trial and there was clear progress. Our headteacher and deputy headteacher came to see it too, so everybody was on the same page and working together. We all understood what we were trying to do, what it was supposed to look and feel like, and then we were able to work on it together. There were a few things to change after that first trial, so I was glad that I had been the one teaching it initially. I think the small steps were probably too small at first, but you live and you learn.

Then, I went to the Year 4 staff and I demonstrated it for them. There is always going to be a mixed bag of reactions, but I believe that teachers are very motivated people and I have never met a teacher who did not want the best for their class. It was my job to support them with the new resources by modelling, team teaching and providing feedback.

Q: How did you roll it out across the trust?

A: We scheduled a session where we invited maths leaders and Year 3 and 4 teachers to come and see the rationale behind it, and explained that we needed to have a consistent, coherent approach. We knew that across our schools, there wasn't a clear system beyond a weekly test, so we all decided to try it. I scheduled a couple of sessions for people to come and observe me in my school. Year 3 and 4 teachers came and saw it in action and took part in a pre- and post-session discussion. We made sure to communicate our intentions and decisions. It was a genuine exchange where people could share their worries, ask questions and understand how it would all work. There were worries about timetables and 'being allowed' to use half a maths lesson a week on times tables, so my next step was to speak to headteachers and share what I had heard. It was important to get them on board and explain the commitment needed from them, and how they could support their teachers with the new resources. I made myself available to go to schools to model the sessions for the teachers.

Q: What is the impact of this work?

A: All of the schools that took part in trialling these resources and committed to the weekly longer sessions and short daily sessions saw an increase in their Multiplication Table Check results. Average scores went up across the board and the schools that had engaged most had the best improvement.

Case study: behaviours – embedding a reasoning progression framework across KS1 and KS2

Maya is the new maths subject leader at a three-form-entry primary school on the outskirts of a large city. She knows that reasoning is on the school improvement plan, but she isn't sure what the current practice looks like as she is new to the school. She works collaboratively with the senior leadership team to embed the behaviours identified by the EEF as central to effective implementation: engaging, uniting and reflecting.

Engaging

To effectively engage the school community, Maya prioritises transparency and co-construction from the beginning. She establishes an implementation team consisting of representatives from every teaching phase, including TAs and a SEND representative. Maya and her SLT recognise that this will be most successful if all areas of the teaching team are represented, and that an investment in time is required to initiate the process. This team serve as a sounding board and a vehicle for shaping decisions. The three teachers (one from EYFS, one from KS1 and one from KS2) are covered by higher level teaching assistants (HLTAs), and the TAs are released from class in order to participate. The first conversation lasts one hour, giving time to explain the rationale. Next, they meet for 20 minutes each fortnight for one term. Maya facilitates structured discussions to gather perspectives on existing practices and concerns about proposed changes. These are not token consultations to appease the team; everyone has input and influences key aspects of the work at hand, such as adaptable sentence stems and classroom talk strategies.

Clear communication is critical. Maya creates a shared digital folder where the implementation rationale, timelines and training resources will be stored and updated. She has a slot in a weekly briefing session with teaching staff to explain that there will be increased focus on reasoning in maths, and to go through the implementation process so that everyone is aware of what is happening, even if they are not directly involved.

Here is the timeline that Maya shares with her staff:

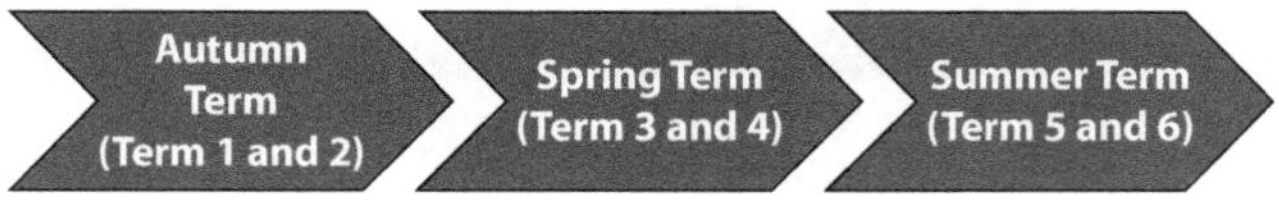

Figure 12.1 Three chevrons showing the progression through the academic year, separated as autumn, spring and summer terms

<table>
<tr>
<td>Weeks 3-4: Subject leader conducts learning walks to gauge current practice in maths lessons.

Week 5: Share findings with SLT and plan implementation.

Week 6: Establish implementation team with representatives across all phases and roles in the school.

Week 7: Meet with the implementation team for one hour session.

Week 8 (after half-term): Briefing for all staff to introduce the implementation plan.

Weeks 9-10: Paired observations (Year 3 teachers) and meet with the implementation team.

Weeks 11-12: Meet with the implementation team and SLT to develop reasoning framework.</td>
<td>Week 2: PD for all teaching staff, using pupil voice and learning walk findings.

Week 4: PD for all teaching staff on reasoning framework with the opportunity to rehearse and refine practice.

Week 5: Trial in class.

Week 6: Continue trialling and feedback via a short online survey.

Weeks 7-8 (after half-term): Subject leader to join PPA and co-plan with teaching teams.

Weeks 9-10: Continue trialling using resources from co-planning sessions.

Week 11: Subject leader and SLT to conduct learning walks.

Week 12: Review point for the implementation team, subject leader and SLT.</td>
<td>Week 2: PD for all teaching staff based on learning walks.

Weeks 3-4: KS1 paired observations.

Weeks 5-6: KS2 paired observations.

Week 7: Feedback to subject leader via a short online survey, followed up with a 15 minute discussion in a PD meeting.

Week 8 (after half-term): Meet with the implementation team and SLT to review and plan ahead for how to embed and sustain next year.</td>
</tr>
</table>

Uniting

Maya knows that staff buy-in hinges on aligning the new initiative with existing values. Instead of positioning the framework as a radical shift, she frames it as a refinement of good practice already happening inconsistently. She runs a PD session focusing on pupil voice, using anonymised transcripts of classroom talk to explore what effective mathematical reasoning sounds like. Staff discuss how developing consistent approaches can reduce workload, improve pupil independence and make assessment more meaningful.

Professional development is designed to unite not just values, but also practices. Teachers rehearse using the new reasoning prompts and receive peer feedback during another after school PD session. Then, Maya organises paired observations for the Year 3 teachers so that they can observe reasoning in action and discuss how the framework works in their year group. These teachers pair up, and register for a date and time that works for them to conduct their paired observations, which happen during the timetabled maths lessons to avoid missing out on other curriculum areas. A mixture of SLT and HLTAs are used to cover these chunks of time.

Reflecting

From the outset, Maya embeds routines for structured reflection. She develops a simple monitoring schedule that includes pupil voice, book looks and informal drop-ins. Staff are encouraged to keep a short reflective log of how reasoning strategies are landing in the classroom, which Maya reviews weekly and uses to adapt training content in real time.

Reflection extends to pupils too. Maya trials a 'reasoning journal' in Year 5, where pupils respond to open-ended prompts once a week. Insights from these journals shape tweaks to sentence stems, and prompt additional scaffold examples for lower-attaining pupils.

Throughout, Maya frames implementation as an evolving process. Rather than striving for immediate perfection, she promotes a culture of ongoing inquiry. Staff understand that feedback loops aren't an evaluation of performance but a mechanism for collective improvement.

2. Attend to the contextual factors that influence implementation

Every school is different. What works brilliantly in one setting may fall flat in another; this is not necessarily because the strategy is flawed, but because it doesn't fit the context. As a maths lead, your implementation plan must reflect your school's unique environment, culture and needs.

Consider the strengths and challenges of your teaching team. Are they confident in their subject knowledge? Do they already have established habits around reasoning or problem solving? Will your changes build on this or require a bigger cultural shift? Equally, think about logistical factors such as time for collaboration, available resources and school routines. If you're introducing something like a new scheme of work or a whole-school approach to fluency, it needs to fit within existing systems or be accompanied by clear, manageable adjustments.

The community you serve is another part of your context. For example, if you plan to engage parents in supporting maths learning at home, consider how accessible your strategies are for the families in your school, thinking about how language barriers, work schedules or previous experiences with maths can all impact the success of your efforts. Attending to context means leading with awareness, adaptability and realism.

Case study: contextual factors

What is being implemented

Maya selects a reasoning framework built on research-informed strategies, including sentence stems, talk tasks and structured problem types. To ensure the framework is appropriate for the school's setting, she conducts a gap analysis of current reasoning provision using book looks, lesson observations and a staff questionnaire. This process confirms that reasoning is being approached inconsistently across year groups, and many teachers lack a shared language or bank of strategies. The selected approach is deliberately designed to be clear, flexible and low on administrative burden, increasing its feasibility for a one-form-entry school.

Systems and structures

Recognising the crucial role of systems in the implementation process, Maya works closely with SLT to embed the new reasoning framework into existing systems. Together, they agree to allocate designated time during regular staff meetings and in-service training (INSET) days for professional development and collaborative planning. Rather than create new monitoring tools, Maya embeds reasoning checkpoints into the school's existing assessment and subject leader forms. She also introduces a section in the medium term plan where teachers can note their use of reasoning strategies, making integration seamless rather than additional.

Importantly, the leadership team agree to adjust timetabling to enable peer observations and coaching sessions focused on reasoning. This requires strategic replanning, but ensures staff can see the framework in action and discuss adaptations in real time. To support sustainability, Maya ensures the initiative is included in the school's improvement plan and subject leader cycle so it remains a monitored priority.

People who enable change

Maya identifies key colleagues to support the implementation effort. She works with two phase leaders to act as early adopters and co-lead coaching conversations within their teams. This distributed leadership ensures that change isn't reliant solely on Maya, and allows each team to adapt the framework within agreed boundaries. She also liaises with the SENDCo to review how reasoning can be scaffolded for pupils with additional needs, and provides tailored resources for TAs involved in small-group work.

To build agency, Maya runs drop-in clinics for teachers to ask questions, trial resources and reflect on what works in their context. She also seeks feedback from staff through informal conversations and anonymous surveys, using this input to refine the approach. Maya ensures all contributors feel empowered, and understand their role in embedding reasoning consistently across the school.

3. Use a structured but flexible implementation process (Explore, Prepare, Deliver, Sustain)

The EEF (Sharples et al., 2024) recommends thinking about implementation as a process with four overlapping and interconnected stages: Explore, Prepare, Deliver and Sustain. This model is especially helpful for maths leaders aiming to embed long-term improvements in their subject.

Explore: Start by identifying the problem you want to solve. Use evidence such as pupil outcomes, staff surveys, book looks or lesson visits to define the issue. Then consider possible approaches, drawing from research, case studies or peer networks. At this stage, it's important to resist jumping to solutions. Focus on understanding the why before choosing the what.

Prepare: Once you've selected your approach, build readiness. This means thinking through logistics, planning professional development, aligning resources and clarifying what success will look like. Prepare your team with clear communication, training and time to plan together. You might pilot a strategy in one year group to gather feedback before rolling it out widely.

Deliver: Put the plan into action with a clear sense of pace and purpose. Provide regular opportunities for teachers to reflect, ask questions and adapt their practice. Offer coaching, model lessons and keep returning to the 'why' so that momentum doesn't slip. Collect qualitative and quantitative evidence to monitor how things are going.

Sustain: Too often, great initiatives fade once the novelty wears off or when staff turnover occurs. Sustaining change means building habits, embedding new practices into the school's routines and continuing to refine based on feedback. Revisit your goals, celebrate successes and make space for the changes to become part of how maths is taught and led, not just a temporary project!

Case study: implementation process

EXPLORE

Step 1: Identify a priority

- Lesson observations and book looks reveal reasoning is often missing or tokenistic.

- Pupil interviews show that they struggle to explain thinking or approach unfamiliar problems.

Step 2: Make evidence-informed decisions on solutions

- Maya reviews guidance from NCETM on mathematical reasoning.
- She attends Maths Hub training and studies other school case studies.
- Maya selects a progression framework with sentence stems and modelling strategies.

Step 3: Examine the fit and feasibility to your context

- Maya pilots the approach in Year 3.
- She gathers weekly teacher feedback and observes lessons.
- The framework proves adaptable to existing planning structures.

PREPARE

Step 4: Develop an implementation plan

- Maya and her SLT create a timeline with PD dates and key review points.
- She delivers an introductory twilight session.
- She plans co-planning sessions during PPA for task refinement.

Step 5: Assess school readiness

- Maya conducts a staff confidence survey on reasoning.
- She holds readiness discussions with SLT.
- They adjust the plan to include more modelling and coaching support.

DELIVER

Step 6: Adopt a flexible and motivating leadership approach

- Maya and SLT take a coaching approach with regular check-ins.
- Maya encourages feedback and celebrates small successes.
- The team promote a non-judgemental, supportive atmosphere.

Step 7: Provide follow-up support

- Maya sets up shared online documents for recording task use.
- She uploads examples of reasoning strategies.
- Maya and SLT organise peer observations and co-teaching partnerships.

Step 8: Use implementation data to actively tailor and improve

- Maya collects data via pupil books, pupil voice and staff reflections.
- She responds to reported challenges (e.g. with arithmetic starters) by creating 'mini-stem' resources.

SUSTAIN

Step 9: Regularly review and decide how to proceed

- Maya leads a review after two terms using book evidence.
- The staff vote to continue using the framework.
- Maya and SLT identify next steps: enrich geometry/statistics examples.

Step 10: Maintain ongoing support and monitoring

- They build reasoning into maths moderation and lesson study cycles.
- Maya adds reasoning materials to the new staff induction training.
- SLT and Maya maintain visibility and support through termly follow-up.

The flexibility of this model lies in its responsiveness because implementation won't always be linear. Some stages may blur or need revisiting, but using this structure can help you avoid common pitfalls and increase the chances that change will stick.

Example implementation plan

Action plans or implementation plans vary from school to school, but it is important to have one. This way, you have a shared strategy document for what you are implementing and you can communicate this with the key stakeholders. However, as implementation is not linear, this should not be a fixed document. It should be flexible and dynamic while remaining structured and planned.

Here is an example implementation plan:

<table>
<tr><td colspan="6">Problem: Mathematical reasoning was inconsistently embedded across classes. Pupils lacked confidence in articulating thinking, and reasoning tasks were often tokenistic.</td></tr>
<tr><td colspan="3">What needs to change?
• Teachers need to explicitly model and embed reasoning strategies.
• Pupils need to explain their thinking confidently and fluently.
• Reasoning should be integrated throughout lessons, not bolted on.</td><td colspan="3">What behaviours will you see when it's working?
• Teachers model reasoning and use prompts regularly.
• Pupils use sentence stems independently.
• Reasoning tasks are embedded within fluency and problem-solving activities.
• There is consistent representation of reasoning across books and classrooms.</td></tr>
<tr><td colspan="6">Intervention: Embedding mathematical reasoning across the curriculum.

Description: A flexible framework including sentence stems, question prompts and a progression pathway. Teachers adapt it to their lessons. It includes structured PD, peer coaching and collaborative planning.</td></tr>
<tr><td colspan="6">Implementation activities</td></tr>
<tr><td colspan="2">Subject leader actions:
• review NCETM guidance on reasoning
• attend Maths Hub workshops
• pilot the framework in Year 3
• identify training needs
• design new staff induction training on reasoning.</td><td colspan="2">Professional development:
• twilight PD with follow-up planning sessions
• responsive PD based on surveys and monitoring
• collaborative planning
• coaching
• peer drop-in observations.</td><td colspan="2">Monitoring:
• learning walks and drop-ins
• book looks alongside pupils or teachers
• pupil voice
• surveys.</td></tr>
<tr><td colspan="6">Implementation outcomes</td></tr>
<tr><td colspan="2">Short-term:
• Teachers report increased confidence (PD feedback forms).
• There is more frequent use of reasoning stems.</td><td colspan="2">Medium-term:
• Pupils articulate reasoning more clearly (pupil voice).
• Books show consistent reasoning integration.</td><td colspan="2">Long-term:
• There are improved outcomes in reasoning-related assessments.
• Staff embed reasoning habits in future planning.</td></tr>
</table>

Questions for reflection

- What changes have been introduced in your school that didn't stick? Why do you think that was?
- How can you involve staff, pupils or parents and carers in shaping a new maths initiative?
- Have you considered your school's systems, routines and constraints before introducing change?
- What could you do next term to better embed a change you're already working on?

Explore further

- The EEF's guidance report *Putting Evidence to work – A School's Guide to Implementation* (2024) by Prof. Jonathan Sharples, Jon Eaton and Jamila Boughelaf: https://d2tic4wvo1iusb.cloudfront.net/production/eef-guidance-reports/implementation/a_schools_guide_to_implementation.pdf
- *Everything Now: resisting the urge to implement too much too soon* (2017) by Phil Stock: https://joeybagstock.wordpress.com/2017/10/27/everything-now-why-we-need-to-resist-the-urge-to-implement-all-that-is-new/
- Evidence for Learning's insights into de-implementation (nd): https://evidenceforlearning.org.au/support-for-implementation/school-planning-and-recovery/de-implementation

Chapter summary

- Effective implementation in maths leadership requires more than introducing a new initiative. It demands careful planning, communication and long-term thinking.
- The EEF's four-stage model (Explore, Prepare, Deliver, Sustain) helps leaders embed change that lasts and adapt it to their school's unique context.
- Avoiding common pitfalls like rushing, overloading or skipping evaluation can improve your chances of success.

- Strong implementation is built on behaviours such as engaging stakeholders, uniting staff around shared goals and embedding routines for reflection and review.
- Attending to contextual factors, including systems, staff strengths, school routines and community needs, ensures the chosen approach fits your setting.
- Implementation is not a linear checklist, but a flexible and ongoing process that requires responsiveness, monitoring and adjustment over time.

Bibliography

Almond, N. (2020), 'Curriculum coherence: how best to do it', in C. Sealy (ed), *The researchED Guide to The Curriculum*. Woodbridge: John Catt. pp. 59-69

Almond, N. (2025a), *What Is Variation Theory? A Guide For Primary Maths Teachers*. Available at: https://thirdspacelearning.com/blog/variation-theory/

Almond, N. (2025b), *Fluency, Reasoning and Problem Solving: What This Looks Like in Every Maths Lesson*. Available at: https://thirdspacelearning.com/blog/fluency-reasoning-problem-solving/.

Barton, C. (2018), *How I Wish I'd Taught Maths: Lessons learned from research, conversations with experts, and 12 years of mistakes*. Woodbridge: John Catt.

Barton, C. (2020), *Reflect, Expect, Check, Explain: Sequences and Behaviour to Enable Mathematical Thinking in the Classroom*. Woodbridge: John Catt.

Barton, C. (n.d.), *Recommended Educational Research Papers for Teachers to Read*. Available at: https://www.mrbartonmaths.com/research/.

Beck, I. L. and McKeown, M. G. (1985), 'Teaching vocabulary: making the instruction fit the goal', in *Educational Perspectives*, 23, (1), 11–15.

Black, P. and Wiliam, D. (1998), *Inside the Black Box: Raising Standards through Classroom Assessment*. London: Sage Publishing.

Black, P. and Wiliam, D. (2018) 'Classroom assessment and pedagogy', *Assessment in Education: Principles, Policy & Practice*, 25(6), pp. 551–575. doi: 10.1080/0969594X.2018.1441807.

Boudett, K. P., City, E. A. and Murnane, R. J. (2013), *Data Wise: A Step-by-Step Guide to Using Assessment Results to Improve Teaching and Learning*. Cambridge, MA: Harvard Education Press.

Bruner, J. S. (1960), *The Process of Education*. Cambridge, MA: Harvard University Press.

Carbonneau, K., Marley, S. C. and Selig, J. P. (2013), 'A meta-analysis of the efficacy of teaching mathematics with concrete manipulatives', in *Journal of Educational Psychology*, 105, (2), 380-400.

Christodoulou, D. (2017), *Making Good Progress? The Future of Assessment for Learning*. Oxford: Oxford University Press.

Clements, D. H. (1999), 'Subitizing: what is it? Why teach it?', in *Teaching Children Mathematics*, 5, (7), 400-405.

Collin, J. and Quigley, A. (2021) *Teacher Feedback to Improve Pupil Learning: Guidance Report*. London: Education Endowment Foundation. Available at: https://files.eric.ed.gov/fulltext/ED615988.pdf.

Dabell, J. (2025), *How To Use Maths Investigations To Develop Mathematical Reasoning At Any Age*. Available at: https://thirdspacelearning.com/blog/maths-investigations-for-ks2-how-to-make-mathematical-detectives/.

Department for Education (DfE) (2013), *The National Curriculum in England: Key Stages 1 and 2 framework document*. Available at: https://assets.publishing.service.gov.uk/media/5a81a9abe5274a2e8ab55319/PRIMARY_national_curriculum.pdf.

Education Endowment Foundation (EEF), *Teaching and Learning Toolkit*. Available at: https://educationendowmentfoundation.org.uk/education-evidence/teaching-learning-toolkit.

Eisenstadt, N. (2016), *Engaging Parents*. Available at: https://www.suttontrust.com/news-opinion/all-news-opinion/engaging-parents/.

Evidence for Learning (nd), 'Insights into de-implementation'. Available at: https://evidenceforlearning.org.au/support-for-implementation/school-planning-and-recovery/de-implementation.

Fletcher-Wood, H. (2018), *Responsive Teaching: Cognitive Science and Formative Assessment in Practice*. London: Routledge.

Foster, C. (2019), 'The fundamental problem with teaching problem solving', in *Mathematics Teaching*, 265, 8–10.

Fuson, K. C., and Briars, D. J. (1990), 'Using a base-ten blocks learning/teaching approach for first- and second-grade place-value and multidigit addition and subtraction', in *Journal for Research in Mathematics Education*, 21, (3), 180–206.

Garry, T. (2020), *Mastery in Primary Mathematics: a Guide for Teachers and Leaders*. London: Bloomsbury.

Gelman, R. and Gallistel, C. (1978), *The Child's Understanding of Number*. Cambridge, MA: Harvard University Press.

Gray, K. (2015) *How Many Legs?* London: Red Fox.

Gu, L., Huang, R. and Marton, F. (2017), 'Teaching with variation: An effective way of mathematics teaching in China', in R. Huang and Y. Li (eds.) *Teaching and Learning Mathematics through Variation*. Rotterdam: Sense Publishers, pp. 13–41.

Harlen, W. (2007), *Assessment of Learning*. London: Sage Publishing.

Hattie, J. and Timperley, H. (2007), 'The power of feedback', in *Review of Educational Research*, 77, (1), 81–112.

Hattie, J. (2009), *Visible Learning: A Synthesis of Over 800 Meta-Analyses Relating to Achievement*. London: Routledge.

Hattie, J. (2012), *Visible Learning for Teachers: Maximizing Impact on Learning*. London: Routledge.

Haylock, D. (2024), *Mathematics Explained for Primary Teachers* (7th edition). London: Sage Publishing.

Henderson, P., Hodgen, J., Foster, C. and Kuchemann, D. (2022) *Improving Mathematics in Key Stages 2 and 3: Guidance Report*. London: Education Endowment Foundation. Available at: https://d2tic4wvo1iusb.cloudfront.net/production/eef-guidance-reports/maths-ks-2-3/EEF-Improving-Mathematics-in-Key-Stages-2-and-3-2022-Update.pdf?v=1741860359.

Hutchinson, J. (2026), *Primary Curriculum Design: Planning for Ofsted's Intent, Implementation and Impact*. Available at: https://thirdspacelearning.com/blog/primary-curriculum-design/.

Jakes, R. (2025), *What Is Fluency In Maths & How Do Schools Develop It?*. Available at: https://thirdspacelearning.com/blog/what-is-fluency-in-maths-definition-ks2/.

Johnson, E. (2025), *Assessment For Learning: Make Sure You Know How To Use It For Optimum Student Progress*. Available at: https://thirdspacelearning.com/blog/assessment-for-learning/.

Kennedy, M. (2016), 'Parsing the practice of teaching', in *Journal of Teacher Education*, 67, (1), 6–17.

Kilpatrick, J., Swafford, J. and Findell, B. (2001), *Adding It Up: Helping Children Learn Mathematics*. Washington, DC: National Academies Press.

Kroll, V.L. (2005) *Equal Shmequal*. Watertown, MA: Charlesbridge.

Lai, M. Y. and Murray, S. (2012), 'Teaching with procedural variation: a Chinese way of promoting deep understanding of mathematics', in *International Journal for Mathematics Teaching and Learning*. 1–25.

Lopresti, A. (1995) *A Place for Zero*. Watertown, MA: Charlesbridge.

Mackle, K., (2016) Tackling Misconceptions in Primary Mathematics. Oxon: Routledge.

Mackle, K. (2020), *Thinking Deeply about Primary Mathematics*. Woodbridge: John Catt.

Marton, F. (2014), *Necessary Conditions of Learning*. New York, NY: Routledge.

Marton, F. and Booth, S. A. (1997), *Learning and Awareness*. Mahwah, NJ: Lawrence Erlbaum Associates Publishers.

Mattock, P. (2019), *Visible Maths*. Carmarthen: Crown House Publishing.

McClure, L. (2014), *Developing Number Fluency – What, Why and How*. Available at: https://nrich.maths.org/articles/developing-number-fluency-what-why-and-how.

McCourt, M. (2019), *Teaching for Mastery*. Woodbridge: John Catt.

McGrane, C. and McCourt, M. (2020), *Mathematical Tasks: The Bridge Between Teaching and Learning*. Woodbridge: John Catt.

Menotti, A. (2012) *How Many Jelly Beans?* San Francisco, CA: Chronicle Books.

Milbourne, A. (2007) *How Big is a Million?* London: Usborne.

Morgan, D. (2025) 'The Five Big Ideas at Primary – Mathematical Thinking'. NCETM. Available at: https://www.ncetm.org.uk/features/the-five-big-ideas-at-primary-mathematical-thinking/

Morgan, E. (2025), *How To Help Primary School Pupils Develop The Maths Language Skills They Need To Succeed In SATs*. Available at https://thirdspacelearning.com/blog/maths-language-skills/.

Mulholland, K. (2021), *The Problem with Problem-Solving in Maths*. Available at: https://educationendowmentfoundation.org.uk/news/eef-blog-the-problem-with-problem-solving-in-maths.

National Centre for Excellence in the Teaching of Mathematics (NCETM) (2014a), *Mathematics glossary for teachers in Key Stages 1 to 3*. Available at: https://www.ncetm.org.uk/media/hpihrj3s/national-curriculum-glossary.pdf.

National Centre for Excellence in the Teaching of Mathematics (NCETM) (2020), *Representations in our Primary Video Lessons*. Available at: https://www.ncetm.org.uk/features/representations-in-our-primary-video-lessons/.

National Centre for Excellence in the Teaching of Mathematics (NCETM) (2022), *Taking on the Role of Maths Lead in a Primary School*. Available at: https://www.ncetm.org.uk/features/taking-on-the-role-of-maths-lead-in-a-primary-school/.

National Centre for Excellence in the Teaching of Mathematics (NCETM) (2024), *The Five Big Ideas – Variation*. Available at: https://www.ncetm.org.uk/features/the-five-big-ideas-variation/.

National Centre for Excellence in the Teaching of Mathematics (NCETM) (2025), *The Five Big Ideas - Fluency*. Available at: https://www.ncetm.org.uk/features/the-five-big-ideas-at-primary-fluency/

Neuschwander, C. (2009) *Sir Cumference and All the King's Tens*. Watertown, MA: Charlesbridge.

Nunes, T., Bryant, P., Sylva, K. and Barros, R. (2009), *Development of Maths Capabilities and Confidence in Primary School*. Available at: https://dera.ioe.ac.uk/id/eprint/11154/1/DCSF-RR118.pdf.

Office for Standards in Education, Children's Services and Skills (Ofsted) (2022), *Research Review Series: English*. Available at: https://www.gov.uk/government/publications/curriculum-research-review-series-english/curriculum-research-review-series-english.

Office for Standards in Education, Children's Services and Skills (Ofsted) (2023), *Coordinating Mathematical Success: the Mathematics Subject Report*. Available at: https://www.gov.uk/government/publications/subject-report-series-maths/coordinating-mathematical-success-the-mathematics-subject-report.

Oxford University Press (OUP), *Building Children's Vocabulary at Home & School: The Oxford Language Report 2023–2024*. Available at: https://fdslive.oup.com/www.oup.com/oxed/wordgap/Oxford_Language_Report_2023-24_Building_Vocabulary_Home.pdf.

Pinczes, E.J. (1993) *One Hundred Hungry Ants*. Boston, MA: Houghton Mifflin Harcourt.

Pólya, G. (2004), *How to Solve It: A New Aspect of Mathematical Method*. Princeton, NJ: Princeton University Press.

Quigley, A. (2018), *Closing the Vocabulary Gap*. London: Routledge.

Riley, A. (2020) 'Six steps for a positive mindset in the maths classroom'. Headteacher Update. Available at: https://www.headteacher-update.com/content/best-practice/six-steps-for-a-positive-mindset-in-the-maths-classroom

Roediger, H. L. and Butler, A. C. (2011), 'The critical role of retrieval practice in long-term retention', in *Trends in Cognitive Sciences*. 15, (1), 20–27.

Rohrer, D. and Taylor, K. (2007), 'The shuffling of mathematics problems improves learning', in *Instructional Science*, 35, (6), 481–498.

Rosenshine, B. (2012), 'Principles of instruction: research-based strategies that all teachers should know', in *American Educator*, 36, (1), 12–19, 39.

Sayre, A.P. and Sayre, J. (2003) *One is a Snail, Ten is a Crab.* London: Walker Books.
Schmidt, W. H., Wang, H. C. and Mcknight, C. (2005), 'Curriculum coherence: an examination of US mathematics and science content standards from an international perspective', in *Journal of Curriculum Studies*, 37, (5), 525–559.
Sharples, J., Eaton, J. and Boughelaf, J. (2024) *A School's Guide to Implementation*. London: Education Endowment Foundation. Available at: https://d2tic4wvo1iusb.cloudfront.net/production/eef-guidance-reports/implementation/a_schools_guide_to_implementation.pdf.
Sherrington, T. (2019). *Rosenshine's Principles in Action*. Woodbridge: John Catt.
Skemp, R.R. (1976), 'Relational Understanding and Instrumental Understanding', Mathematics Teaching, 77, pp. 20–26. Available at: https://www.atm.org.uk/write/mediauploads/resources/richard_skemp.pdf.
Stiggins, R. (2002), 'Assessment crisis: the absence of assessment FOR learning', in *Phi Delta Kappan*, 83, (10), 758–765.
Stobart, G. (2008), *Testing Times: the Uses and Abuses of Assessment*. London: Routledge.
Stock, P. (2017) 'Everything now: why we need to resist the urge to implement all that is new'. *joeybagstock* (blog). Available at: https://joeybagstock.wordpress.com/2017/10/27/everything-now-why-we-need-to-resist-the-urge-to-implement-all-that-is-new/.
Sweller, J. (1988), 'Cognitive load during problem solving: effects on learning', in *Cognitive Science*, (12), 257–285.
Training & Technical Assistance Center (2022) 'Promoting a math-positive school culture'. Available at: https://ttac.odu.edu/product/promoting-a-math-positive-school-culture/.
Watson, A. and Mason, J. (2006), 'Seeing an exercise as a single mathematical object: using variation to structure sense-making', in *Mathematical Thinking and Learning*, 8, (2), 91–111.
Wiliam, D. (2011), *Embedded Formative Assessment*. Bloomington, IN: Solution Tree Press.
Wiliam, D. (2013), *Principled Curriculum Design*. London: SSAT (Schools Network). Available at: https://webcontent.ssatuk.co.uk/wp-content/uploads/2023/12/05151905/SSAT-Redesigning-Schooling-03-Principled-curriculum-design.pdf.
Wiliam, D. and Leahy, S. (2015), *Embedding Formative Assessment: Practical Techniques for K–12 Classrooms*. Bloomington, IN: Solution Tree Press.
Willatt, M. (2025) 'Maths Problem Solving: Engaging Your Students and Strengthening Their Mathematical Skills'. Third Space Learning. Available at: https://thirdspacelearning.com/blog/maths-problem-solving/
Willingham, D. (2009), *Why Don't Students Like School?*. Hoboken, NJ: Jossey-Bass.
Willingham, D.T. (2017) 'Ask the Cognitive Scientist: Do Manipulatives Help Students Learn?', *American Educator*, 41(3), pp. 25–29. Available at: https://www.aft.org/sites/default/files/ae_fall2017_willingham.pdf

Index